Fairy Time Knits

Fairy Time Knits

AMY CARROLL AND DENISE BROWN

DORLING KINDERSLEY • LONDON

Special thanks to Mrs Hilda Keen and
Mrs Hilda E. Stump for their much appreciated
work in knitting all the sweaters.

Thanks also to Sue Smith and Shirley Bakey at
Babouska Ltd., for their lovely fairytale
button designs to go with the sweaters.
All button designs are copyright.

Editorial Christiane Gunzi

Design Sally Powell

Production Henrietta Winthrop

Photography Fiona Alison

Illustration Sally Kindberg

Backdrops Sophie Kelly

First published in Great Britain in 1988
by Dorling Kindersley Limited,
9 Henrietta Street, London WC2E 8PS
Copyright © 1988
Dorling Kindersley Limited
Sweater designs copyright ©
Amy Carroll and Denise Brown

Printed by Lee Fung Asco, Hong Kong
Typeset by Chambers Wallace, London
Colour reproduction by Hong Kong Graphic Arts

Fairy time knits.
1. Children's sweaters.
Knitting – Patterns
I. Carroll, Amy.   II. Brown,
Denise
646.4′5406

ISBN 0-86318-326-3

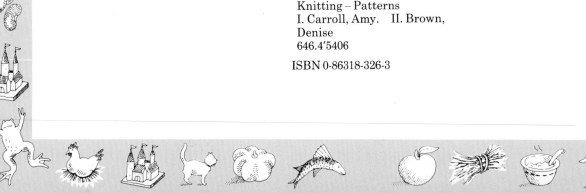

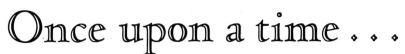

Once upon a time . . .

Once upon a time fairy tale characters were found only in books. Now, the heros and heroines of your child's favourite stories have been captured on 12 new and original sweater designs. Your child can easily choose the design he or she is most eager to wear by looking through the book and reading the fairy tales that accompany each of the sweaters.

The pages immediately following each design give you detailed instructions on how to make the sweater, including the colours used and the quantities of each one required, together with a pattern chart for you to follow for each sweater design.

Our charts have been drawn to accurately reflect knitted fabric (each stitch is a rectangle rather than a square), so what you see on the chart is what the finished pattern actually looks like.

The colourful sweaters have been designed in EMU Double Knitting yarn (the distributors of which are listed on p.64). If you wish, however, you can use any standard yarn that uses 23 stitches and 30 rows to produce a 4-inch (10cm) square on 4mm needles in stocking (stockinette) stitch. On every instruction page, colourful yarn swatches will help you to match up the shade of yarn that you require.

The basic sweater pattern has been designed to accommodate all children by having a large neck opening. This is secured by three buttons on the shoulder opening. You might like to order the special buttons designed by Baboushka Ltd that we commissioned especially for the book, although any 16mm buttons will do.

The basic sweater pattern (p.64) can be made up in three different sizes. You should note that the sizes given (in inches and centimetres) are the finished measurements of the garment, rather than the actual chest measurements of the child. Therefore, make certain to choose the size that will allow sufficient growing room for your child.

Different embroidery techniques are used in order to create specific details, such as the wolf's glinting eye and the little pig's snout. The techniques for creating these stitches, such as French knots and Stem stitch are illustrated with the sweater patterns.

The last ten pages of the book (pp.54-64) contain handy tips on knitting techniques and equipment, and also explain how to use the pattern charts. In addition, there is a special colour guide to working with yarns on pp.56-57.

The Three Little Pigs

Based on the traditional folktale as retold by Joseph Jacobs

There were once three Little Pigs who lived with their mother, until the day when they grew too big for her house.

"You must leave here and build your own houses," their mother told them. So off they all went, and each Little Pig thought about what sort of house he would like to build.

The first Little Pig met a man walking down the road with a great bundle of straw on his back. The Little Pig thought he would like to build his house out of straw, and the man kindly gave him some. That afternoon he built himself a pretty little straw house.

The second Little Pig met a man walking down the road carrying a large load of sticks, so he asked if he could have some to build his little house with. The man gave him a bundle, and the Little Pig built himself a smart house of sticks.

The third Little Pig trotted down the road and met a man pushing a wheelbarrow full of bricks, so he asked if he could have some. The man gave him a big pile of bricks, and the Little Pig worked for days building himself a strong little house, with a door, two windows and a chimney on the roof. When he had finished, the third Little Pig felt very pleased with his work, and went inside to make his dinner.

A few days later, the big, bad Wolf came snooping about and saw the pretty little house of straw with the Little Pig inside.

"Little Pig, Little Pig, let me come in," said the Wolf.

"No, no" said the Little Pig. "By the hair of my chinny chin chin, I won't let you come in."

"Then I'll huff and I'll puff, and I'll blow your house in," said the big bad Wolf. So the Wolf huffed and he puffed, and he blew the little straw house down. The Little Pig squealed and ran all the way to the little house of sticks.

The next day, the Wolf came along the road again and saw the little house of sticks.

"Little Pig, Little Pig, let me come in," said the big bad Wolf.

"No, no" said the two Little Pigs, "By the hair of our chinny chin chins, we won't let you in."

"Then I'll huff and I'll puff, and I'll blow your house in," said the big bad Wolf. So the Wolf huffed and he puffed, and he blew the little house of sticks down. The two Little Pigs both squealed and ran as fast as they could to the house made of bricks where the other Little Pig lived. The Wolf followed them to the brick house (which now had three Little Pigs inside), and he knocked loudly on the door.

"Little Pig, Little Pig, let me come in," said the big bad Wolf.

"No, no," said the three Little Pigs, "By the hair of our chinny chin chins, we won't let you come in."

"Then I'll huff and I'll puff, and I'll blow your house in," said the big bad Wolf. So he huffed and he puffed, and he huffed and puffed again, but however hard he blew, he could not blow the little brick house down.

The big bad Wolf became very angry, and prowled around the house, looking to see if he could find another way inside. Then the Wolf began to climb up the outside of the little brick house, to the roof. The three Little Pigs were very frightened, and they quickly ran and filled a pot with water to put on to the fire. The big bad Wolf climbed on to the roof and looked down the chimney, but as he started to climb down, he slipped and fell right into the pot of boiling water. The Little Pigs rushed to put the lid on the pot, and that was the end of the Wolf. The three Little Pigs would never have to be afraid of that big bad Wolf again.

The Three Little Pigs

Lower ribbing Warm Brown

Front of sweater After working the ribbing in Warm Brown, follow the chart opposite for the picture of the little pig at work. Remember, purl rows are left to right, and knit rows are right to left. Work the top ribbing in Baby Blue.

Back of sweater Work the lower ribbing and the lower half of the back in Warm Brown, changing to Bright Green as on the chart, then work the rest of the back in Baby Blue, omitting the pig, brick wall and shovel.

Sleeves After working the lower ribbing in Warm Brown, work the entire sleeve in Bright Green, including the top ribbing.

Neckband Off White

Buttonstand Baby Blue

Left shoulder opening Work in Baby Blue, changing to Off White when you reach the neckband (see p.64 for buttonhole instructions).

Finishing When the sweater is completed, outline the pig's arm and snout in Backstitch (see right), using Warm Brown. Using Black, work two French knots for the eyes (see p.32). Sew three buttons on to the buttonstand.

Backstitch

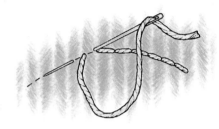

First make a single stitch forward, then bring the thread back underneath the fabric, emerging at a distance of one stitch behind the first one. Re-insert the needle just behind the first stitch, pull the thread through from below, and repeat as necessary.

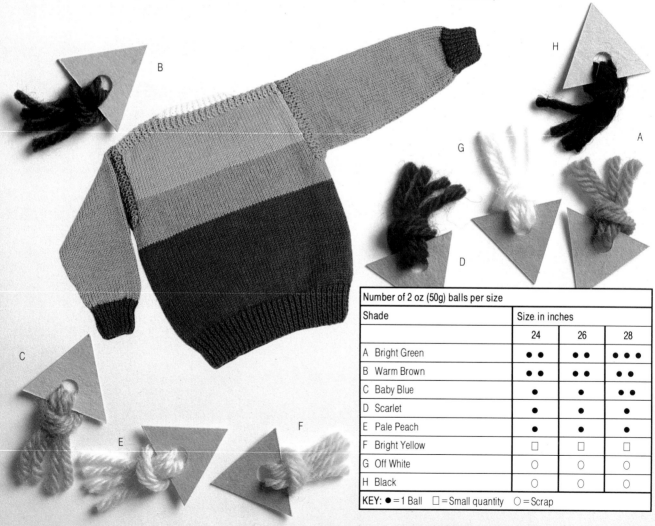

Number of 2 oz (50g) balls per size			
Shade	Size in inches		
	24	26	28
A Bright Green	● ●	● ●	● ● ●
B Warm Brown	● ●	● ●	● ●
C Baby Blue	●	●	● ●
D Scarlet	●	●	●
E Pale Peach	●	●	●
F Bright Yellow	□	□	□
G Off White	○	○	○
H Black	○	○	○
KEY: ● = 1 Ball □ = Small quantity ○ = Scrap			

"The man gave him a big pile of bricks, and the little pig worked for days building himself a strong little house, with a door, two windows and a chimney on the roof."

The Little Mermaid

Based on the fairy tale by Hans Christian Andersen

Once upon a time, in the deepest part of the sea, there lived a little mermaid. When her fifteenth birthday came, she was allowed to swim to the surface to watch the ships go by. The first thing she saw was the wide open sky, and seagulls flying by. A ship lay on the water, its full sails billowing in the breeze. The Little Mermaid swam up to the porthole, and saw people inside eating and drinking together. She listened as they laughed and sang with the young Captain of the ship.

As night approached, the wind blew stronger, until the waves began to splash up against the ship, crashing down on the people inside. Lightning flashed, breaking the ship into fragments. The Little Mermaid saw the young Captain fall into the sea, and darted forward to save him from drowning. Gently she towed him in towards the beach, where she laid him down on the sand. All night long she sat with him, and when morning came, he opened his eyes and smiled, just as his men on horseback came galloping along the beach. Quick as a flash, the Little Mermaid dived into the water and back home to her sea palace.

Many times she swam to the surface, but there was no sign of the handsome Captain, until one day her sisters told her that he was the Prince who lived in the castle on the cliff. From that day on, she often came to sit on the rock to look up at the castle. The Prince in his castle often wondered what had happened to the pretty girl who had rescued him from the sea.

As time went on, the Little Mermaid longed to visit the Prince, and wished that she had real legs instead of a tail. She decided to ask the Sea Witch to make a magic potion for her. The Witch agreed to give her human legs in exchange for her tail, but she was greedy, and in payment for the spell, she wanted the Little Mermaid's beautiful voice. The Little Mermaid wanted to meet the Prince again so much that she agreed. As soon as she drank the magic potion, she fell fast asleep.

When the Little Mermaid awoke, she was lying on the beach, and standing next to her was the handsome Prince. She looked down at her tail and saw two little white legs there instead. The Prince asked her who she was, but she could not tell him, so he took her to his castle, where he gave her little slippers for her feet. As the weeks passed, the two friends became very fond of each other. The Prince loved the Little Mermaid for her sweet and gentle nature, but he did not wish to marry her. He told her that he would only marry the girl who had found him on the beach after the terrible storm. The Little Mermaid wept because she had saved his life but he would never know.

One day, the King announced that the Prince would marry the Princess in the next kingdom. The Prince was angry and miserable, and said he could not marry someone he did not love. But when he met the Princess and saw how lovely she was, he fell in love with her.

The Little Mermaid wandered sadly along the beach, but stopped when she heard singing. There, in the water, were all her sisters, but they were shorn of their flowing hair. They told the Little Mermaid that they had sold it all to the Sea Witch in exchange for a magic knife. With this knife the Little Mermaid could kill the Prince, and return to the sea palace. The Little Mermaid took the magic knife, but she could not kill the man she loved, and threw it away into the ocean.

That night there was a wonderful celebration for the royal wedding, and the Little Mermaid danced as gracefully as anyone. But in the morning she hurled herself into the sea. The spirits of the air took pity on the unhappy Mermaid. They carried her up to heaven, where she lived happily ever after doing good deeds.

The Little Mermaid

Lower ribbing Pale Lemon

Front of sweater After working the ribbing in Pale Lemon, follow the chart opposite for the picture of the Mermaid. Remember, purl rows are left to right, and knit rows are right to left. Work the top ribbing in Ice Blue.

Back of sweater Work the lower ribbing in Pale Lemon, joining in the Royal Blue as for the front. Then change to Ice Blue as on chart, omitting the Mermaid, rocks, fish and sun. Work the top ribbing in Ice Blue.

Sleeves After working the lower ribbing in Pale Lemon, join in the Royal Blue to make waves, as on the chart. Continue in

Royal Blue until the sleeve measures 6½/7/7in (17/18/18cm). Then change to Ice Blue and work the rest of the sleeve (including the top ribbing) to the required length for your size.

Neckband and Buttonstand Ice Blue

Left shoulder opening Ice Blue (see p.64 for buttonhole instructions).

Finishing Once the sweater is completed, add the eyes and mouth to the Little Mermaid's face. Using Royal Blue, work two French knots for her eyes (see p. 32), and using Scarlet, work a Cross stitch for her mouth. With Pale Lemon, Swiss darn (Duplicate stitch) the starfish (see right). Sew three buttons on to the buttonstand.

Swiss darning (Duplicate stitch) – working horizontally

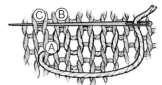

Secure the embroidery yarn at the back of the work and bring your needle out to the front of the work at A. Insert the needle at B, under the base of the stitch above, and bring it out at C. Insert the needle at D and emerge at E ready to embroider the next stitch.

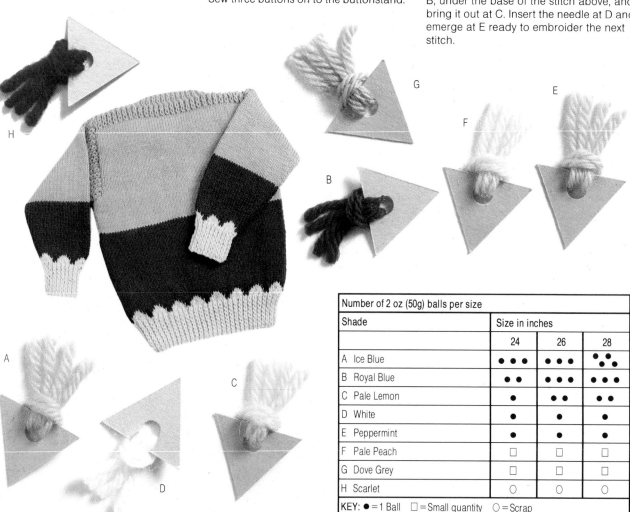

Number of 2 oz (50g) balls per size			
Shade	Size in inches		
	24	26	28
A Ice Blue	● ● ●	● ● ●	● ● ● ● ●
B Royal Blue	● ●	● ● ●	● ● ● ●
C Pale Lemon	●	● ●	● ●
D White	●	●	●
E Peppermint	●	●	●
F Pale Peach	□	□	□
G Dove Grey	□	□	□
H Scarlet	○	○	○
KEY: ● =1 Ball □ =Small quantity ○ =Scrap			

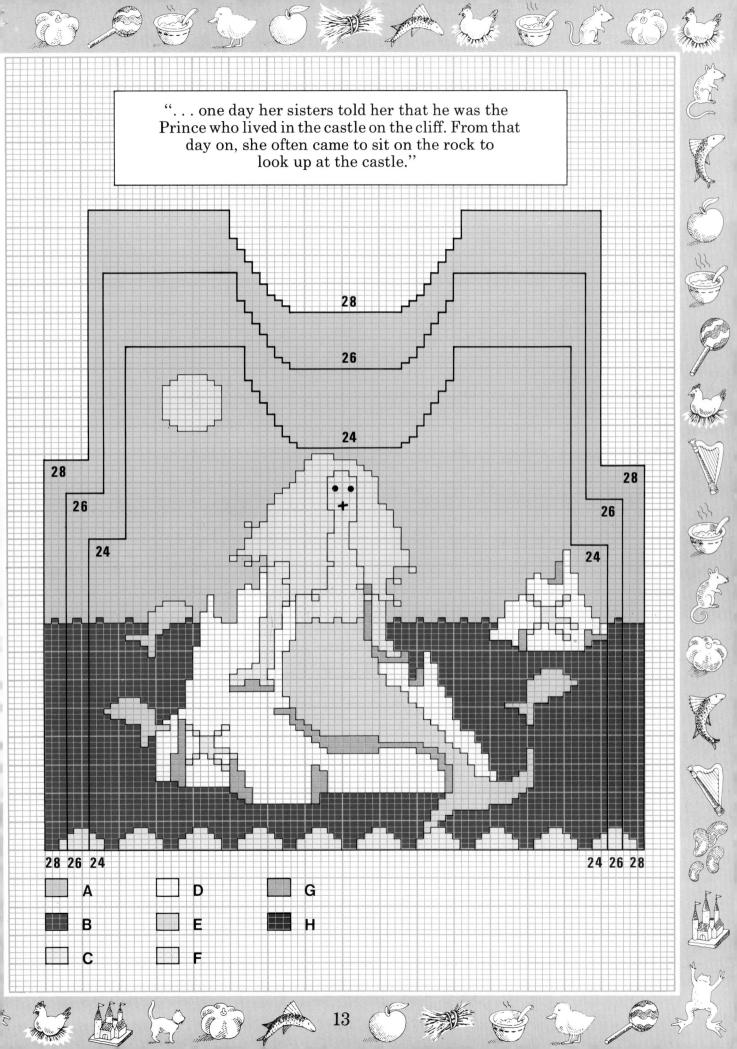

"... one day her sisters told her that he was the Prince who lived in the castle on the cliff. From that day on, she often came to sit on the rock to look up at the castle."

28

26

24

28

26

24

28

26

24

28 26 24

24 26 28

	A		D		G
	B		E		H
	C		F		

Jack and The Beanstalk

Based on the traditional folktale as retold by Joseph Jacobs

There was once a boy called Jack, who went to market to sell his mother's cow because they had no food left. On the way, a strange old man offered him some shiny coloured beans in exchange for the cow. When Jack saw how beautiful and bright the beans were, he could not resist them, and sold the man his cow. When Jack's mother discovered what he had done, she was furious, and threw the beans out of the window. Now they had no cow, no milk and no money.

Jack worried all night and did not sleep well. But the next day when he looked out of his window, he could not believe his eyes. Outside, a great beanstalk was reaching high up into the sky for as far as he could see. Jack rushed downstairs into the garden. Up the beanstalk he went, grabbing hold of the stalks and climbing higher and higher, until all the houses looked like little dots below. At last he reached the top.

There, Jack found himself in a strange land. In front of him was an enormous castle. Jack was so hungry after his long climb that he knocked on the door to ask for some food. An old lady shouted from inside,
"Go away, go away, my husband will eat you if he finds you here." But Jack would not listen, so the old woman let him in to have some food. As Jack was eating, there was the most dreadfully loud thump, thump, thump of footsteps outside. Just in time, the woman bundled Jack into the oven to hide. As she closed the oven door Jack heard the terrible voice of the Giant.
"Fe, fi, fo, fum, I smell the blood of an Englishman. Be he alive or be he dead, I'll grind his bones to make my bread."
"Nonsense," said his brave little wife, "it's your supper that you can smell, so sit down here and eat it before it gets cold."
When the Giant had finished his meal, his wife brought his hen that laid eggs of pure gold. Every time he told the hen to lay an egg, it did, and Jack could see the pile of golden eggs as he peeped out of the oven.

Later, when the Giant was sleeping, Jack crept out, grabbed the hen, and ran as fast as his legs would carry him back to the beanstalk. Down and down he scrambled, until at last he reached the ground where his mother was waiting. From then on they lived happily with the hen that laid golden eggs.

A few months later, when Jack felt brave and adventurous, he decided to climb the beanstalk again. Up and up he went, until he reached the Giant's castle. He crept up to an open window and peeped in to see the Giant eating his supper. When he had finished, the little old lady brought a harp, and when the Giant commanded it to play, the most beautiful music that you ever heard came floating through the house. The music soon sent the Giant to sleep, so Jack climbed in through the window to steal the harp. Just as he picked it up, the harp squeaked.
"Master, master, wake up!" The noise woke the terrible Giant, who roared when he saw Jack. He tried to catch him, but Jack slipped through his fingers, and sped out of the castle, down the road, to the top of the beanstalk, clutching the harp. Down he climbed as fast as he could, with the Giant chasing after him.
"Quickly Mother, hurry," Jack shouted when he was close to his house, "Fetch me my axe!" As soon as Jack reached the ground, he grabbed the axe and began chopping away at the beanstalk. He chopped and chopped as fast as he could, until at last the beanstalk began to sway. Down to the ground crashed the Giant and the beanstalk. The Giant was killed and that was the end of him and the beanstalk.

Jack and The Beanstalk

Lower ribbing Warm Brown

Front of sweater After working the ribbing in Warm Brown, follow the chart opposite for the picture of Jack climbing down the beanstalk. Remember, purl rows are left to right, and knit rows are right to left. Work the top ribbing in colours and numbers of stitches to match the chart.

Back of sweater Work the lower ribbing in Warm Brown, then follow the chart for five rows to make the beanstalk pattern running across the lower part of the sweater. Continue in Powder Blue for the rest of the back. Work the top ribbing in Pale Lemon.

Sleeves After working the lower ribbing in Warm Brown, work five rows of beanstalk

pattern as for the back, then change to Powder Blue for the rest of the sleeve, including the top ribbing.

Neckband Lime Green

Buttonstand Powder Blue

Left shoulder opening Follow the chart for the pattern and colours, changing to Lime Green when you reach the neckband (see p.64 for buttonhole instructions).

Finishing Once the sweater is completed, work the axe in White and Warm Brown Satin stitch. Sew three buttons on to the buttonstand.

Satin stitch – working horizontally

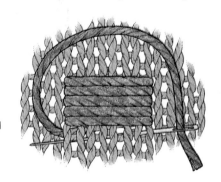

To obtain the best results, work evenly in horizontal stitches. The stitches should fit closely together, giving a very smooth surface and straight outside edges.

Number of 2 oz (50g) balls per size			
Shade	Size in inches		
	24	26	28
A Powder Blue	● ● ●	● ● ● ●	● ● ● ● ●
B Warm Brown	●	● ●	● ●
C Dark Green	●	●	● ●
D Lime Green	●	●	●
E White	●	●	●
F Pale Lemon	●	●	●
G Bright Yellow	●	●	●
H Flame Red	□	□	□
I Black	□	□	□
J Pale Peach	○	○	○
KEY: ● =1 Ball □ =Small quantity ○ =Scrap			

16

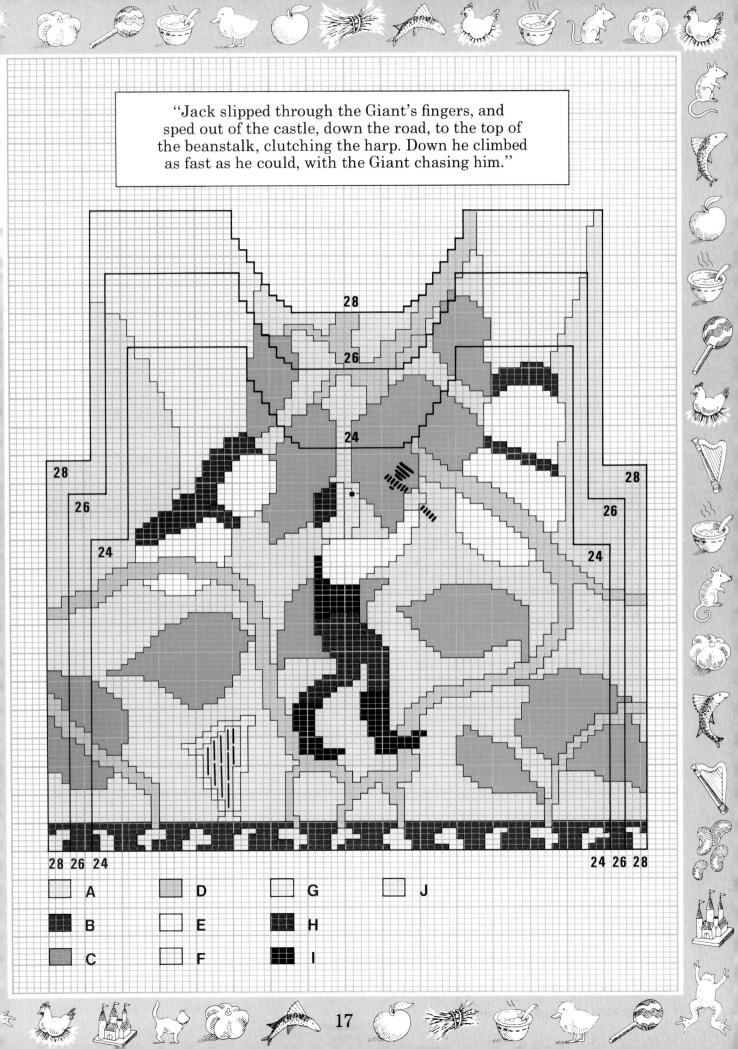

"Jack slipped through the Giant's fingers, and
sped out of the castle, down the road, to the top of
the beanstalk, clutching the harp. Down he climbed
as fast as he could, with the Giant chasing him."

28

26

24

28

26

24

28

26

24

28

26

24

28 26 24

24 26 28

A   D   G   J

B   E   H

C   F   I

Goldilocks and The Three Bears

Based on the traditional folktale as retold by Joseph Jacobs

In the deepest part of the woods there was a cottage in which lived three bears. There was a small, wee, Baby Bear, a middle-sized Mother Bear and a great, big Father Bear. Every morning the three bears had a pot of porridge for their breakfasts. There was a little bowl for the small, wee Baby Bear, a medium-sized bowl for the Mother Bear and a large bowl for the great, big Father Bear.

Each of them had a chair to sit on. There was a little chair for the small, wee Baby Bear, a medium-sized chair for the Mother Bear, and a great big chair for the big Father Bear. Each of the bears had a bed to sleep in. The small, wee Baby Bear had a little bed, the Mother Bear had a middle-sized bed, and the big, huge Father Bear had a great, big bed.

One day, after making the pot of porridge, the three bears set off for a walk while their porridge was cooling, leaving the front door open.

Now, in the woods there also lived a little girl. She had long golden hair down to her waist, so she was called Goldilocks. That morning, while the three bears were out walking, Goldilocks went to play in the woods on her own. She was skipping along the path when, all of a sudden, she spotted the little house with its open door. Goldilocks could smell the porridge, so she wandered in. Inside, she saw three bowls on the table.

First she tasted the porridge in the great, big bowl, but it was too hot. Next she tasted the porridge in the medium-sized bowl, but it was too cold. Then she tasted the porridge in the small bowl. That was just right, so she gobbled it up.

Goldilocks was so full of porridge that she soon began to feel sleepy, and went to sit on a chair. First she tried to sit on the great, big chair, but it was too high for her. Then she sat on the medium-sized chair but that was too low for her, so then she tried the little chair. Goldilocks squeezed herself in, but the bottom fell out, and she found herself sitting on the floor.

Goldilocks became very cross, and went upstairs to see if there was a comfortable bed on which to lie. First she lay down on the great, big bed, but it was too hard for her, so then she lay down on the medium-sized bed, but that was too soft for her. Finally, she tried the littlest bed, and that was just right, and she soon fell asleep.

Soon the hungry bears came home for their breakfasts. The house was not as they had left it. "Who's been eating my porridge?" asked the great, big Father Bear in his loud gruff voice.

"And who's been eating my porridge?" asked the Mother Bear in her medium sort of voice.

"And who's been eating my porridge?" piped the small, wee Baby Bear in his high little voice, "because they've eaten it all up!" The three bears then looked further around the room.

"Who's been sitting in my chair?" growled the great, big Father Bear.

"And who's been sitting in my chair?" asked the Mother Bear.

"And who's been sitting in my chair?" sobbed the small, wee Baby Bear, "because they've sat the bottom out of it!"

The three bears went upstairs.

"Who's been sleeping in my bed?" said the great, big Father Bear in his rough, gruff voice.

"And who's been sleeping in my bed?" said the Mother Bear, looking at the squashed pillow.

"And who's been sleeping in my bed?" squeaked the small, wee Baby Bear in astonishment, "and she's still there!" At that moment Goldilocks awoke. She saw the three bears standing around the bed and screamed in fright. She leapt out of bed and out of the house, and that was the last the three bears ever saw of Goldilocks.

Goldilocks and The Three Bears

Lower ribbing Mauve

Front of sweater After working the ribbing in Mauve, follow the chart on the page opposite for the picture of Goldilocks and the bears. Remember, purl rows are left to right, and knit rows are right to left. Work the top ribbing in Cream.

Back of sweater Work the lower ribbing in Mauve, then work all of the back in Cream, including the top ribbing.

Sleeves After working the lower ribbing in Mauve, work the entire sleeve in Cream, including the top ribbing.

Neckband and Buttonstand Cream

Left shoulder opening Cream (see p.64 for buttonhole instructions).

Finishing To complete the picture, embroider the bedspread in White using Stem stitch (see right). For the bears' eyes, use Chocolate Brown French knots (see p.32), and for their noses, use Chocolate Brown and Satin stitch (see p.16). Outline their mouths and chins in Backstitch and Chocolate Brown (see p.8). Then using Baby Blue, Swiss darn ([Duplicate stitch] see p.12) two eyes on to Goldilocks, and in Flame Red and Satin stitch, work her mouth. Sew three buttons on to the buttonstand.

Stem stitch

Work the stitch with the thread kept on the same side of the needle. For a wider effect, insert the needle into the ground fabric at a slight angle. The greater the angle, the wider the effect.

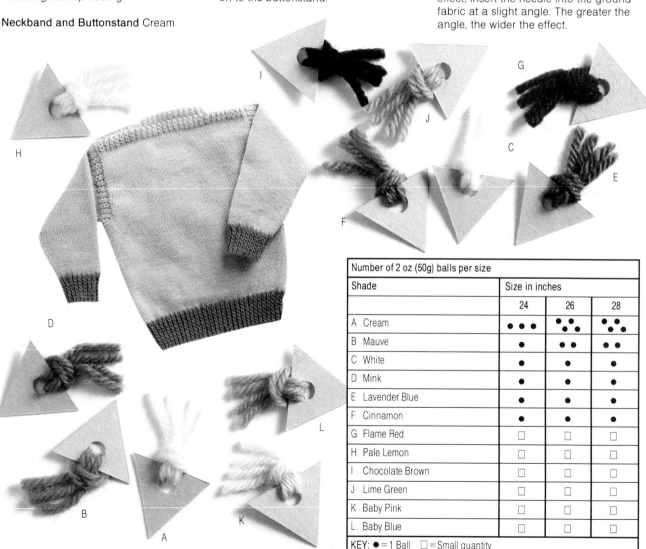

Number of 2 oz (50g) balls per size			
Shade	Size in inches		
	24	26	28
A Cream	● ● ●	● ● ●	● ● ●
B Mauve	●	● ●	● ●
C White	●	●	●
D Mink	●	●	●
E Lavender Blue	●	●	●
F Cinnamon	●	●	●
G Flame Red	□	□	□
H Pale Lemon	□	□	□
I Chocolate Brown	□	□	□
J Lime Green	□	□	□
K Baby Pink	□	□	□
L Baby Blue	□	□	□
KEY: ● =1 Ball □ =Small quantity			

"At that moment Goldilocks awoke. She saw the three bears standing around the bed and screamed in fright. She leapt out of bed and out of the house."

Puss in Boots

Based on the traditional fairy tale as retold by Charles Perrault

There was once a miller's son who was miserable because all he had was a cat, and he thought he would never be rich. But the Puss was no ordinary cat, and said to his master,
"If you give me a pair of gentlemen's boots, and a sack to catch rabbits in, I will make you a rich man." The Miller's Son was amazed to hear the cat speak, and bought him the finest boots that he could find. Off went Puss in Boots to catch rabbits, and when he had a bagful, he took it to the King. He said the rabbits were from the Marquis of Carabas (which was a name that he had invented). The King was delighted, and gave him a saucer of cream.

A few days later, the cat heard that the King was going for a drive with his daughter, the Princess. Puss in Boots rushed to his master and told him to go for a swim in the river. The Miller's Son thought this was a strange idea, but he felt like a swim, so off he went. While he was in the water, the King's carriage came along, and Puss in Boots started to shout and yell,
"Help, help, the Marquis of Carabas is drowning!" All the King's soldiers rushed to save the Miller's son. Puss in Boots told them that thieves had robbed his master, so a footman was ordered to bring clothes and a horse from the palace. Soon the Footman returned on a fine white mare, carrying an elegant suit of silk and velvet.

Puss in Boots was so pleased with himself that he ran all the way to the next field where peasants were harvesting corn. He leapt on to the gate and shouted to everyone,
"The King is coming, and you must all pretend that this land belongs to the Marquis of Carabas. If not, you will all be chopped into mincemeat!" The peasants were afraid, and did what they were told. When the King drove by, he said in surprise,
"You have some excellent crops growing in your fields, Marquis." The Miller's Son just smiled. Puss in Boots chuckled to himself, and ran on to the castle where the Ogre lived. He was enormous, and could change into anything that he wanted to, so he was very frightening. Puss in Boots had never met an ogre before, but he was a brave cat, and felt even braver in his smart boots, so he marched up to the castle and knocked on the door. The Ogre was surprised to see a puss in boots, and he was even more surprised when the cat began to speak, so he was invited in.
"My dear Ogre, I have heard that you can change your shape!" In an instant the Ogre had changed into a hungry lion and roared loudly. Puss in Boots jumped in fright and leapt up the chimney to hide. After a while, when all was quiet, he peeped out and saw that the Ogre had changed back into himself.
"My goodness!" said Puss in Boots "How clever you are! However, I bet you can't change into something tiny like a mouse."
"Of course I can" bellowed the Ogre, and in a flash, all that was left was a little white mouse. Quick as a flash, Puss in Boots pounced, and ate it up, and that was the end of the Ogre.

At that moment, the King's carriage passed close to the castle, and Puss in Boots hurried to the front gates, bowing low as it passed by.
"Welcome, your Majesty, to the castle of the Marquis of Carabas." The King, the Princess and the Miller's Son were all astonished, but the Miller's Son covered up his surprise, and invited the King and his daughter to dinner. The King so enjoyed the splendid meal, that he offered the Princess's hand in marriage to the Miller's Son. Puss in Boots was knighted by the King. He lived as a lord with the Princess and the Miller's Son in the Ogre's castle, and he never had to catch rabbits again.

Puss in Boots

Lower ribbing Turquoise

Front of sweater After working the ribbing in Turquoise, follow the chart opposite for the picture of Puss in Boots. Remember, purl rows are left to right, and knit rows are right to left. For the top ribbing, continue the panels in Turquoise, using White on the remaining stitches as necessary.

Back of sweater Work the lower ribbing in Turquoise, then follow the chart as for the front, omitting Puss in Boots. For the top ribbing, continue to work the panels in Turquoise, using White on the remaining stitches as necessary.

Sleeves After working the lower ribbing in Turquoise, work the entire sleeve in White, including the top ribbing.

Neckband and Buttonstand White

Left shoulder opening Pick up and knit stitches as directed in the pattern, keeping the eleven Turquoise stitches as on the front of sweater (see p.64 for buttonhole instructions).

Finishing Once the sweater is completed, add whiskers to the face of Puss in Boots in Black. Sew three buttons on to the buttonstand.

Keeping colours separate

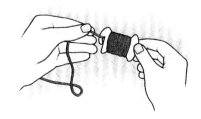

When working multiple colour patterns such as this one, it often happens that the different yarns get tangled. To keep this from happening, wind manageable lengths of yarn on to bobbins, yarn holders or spools. Short lengths of yarn can then be unwound as you work.

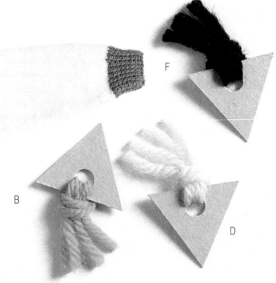

Number of 2 oz (50g) balls per size			
Shade	Size in inches		
	24	26	28
A White	● ● ● ●	● ● ●	● ● ● ●
B Turquoise	● ●	● ●	● ● ●
C Scarlet	●	●	●
D Pale Lemon	●	●	●
E Dark Grey	●	●	●
F Black	□	□	□
G Jade Green	○	○	○
KEY: ● = 1 Ball □ = Small quantity ○ = Scrap			

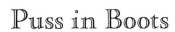

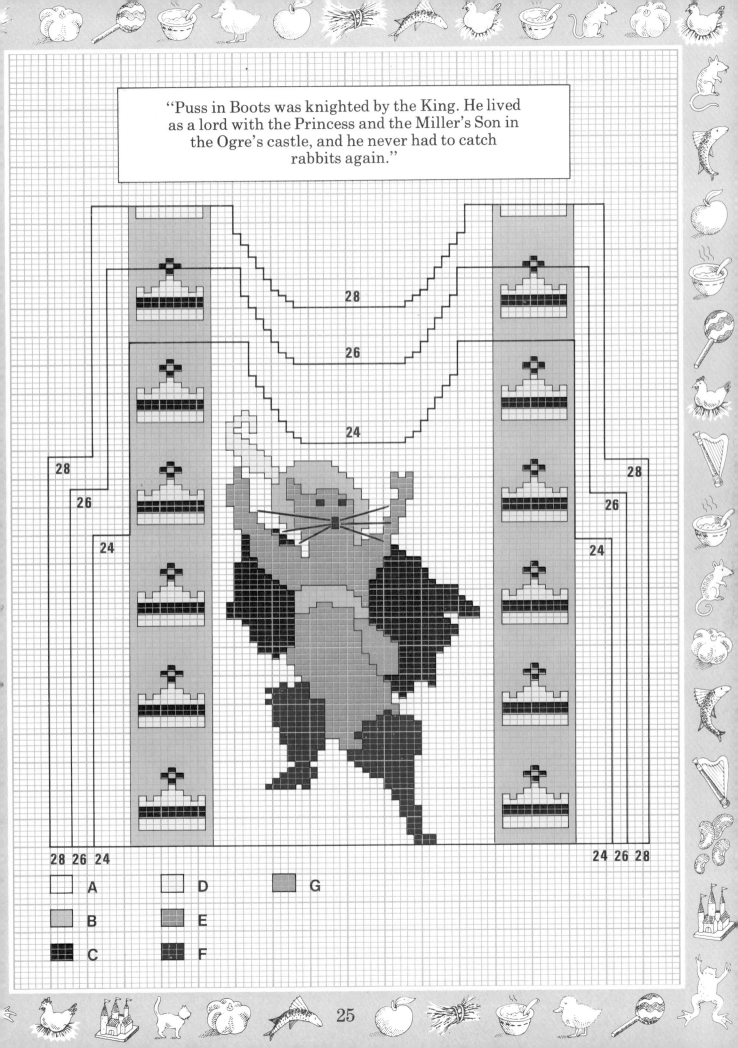

"Puss in Boots was knighted by the King. He lived as a lord with the Princess and the Miller's Son in the Ogre's castle, and he never had to catch rabbits again."

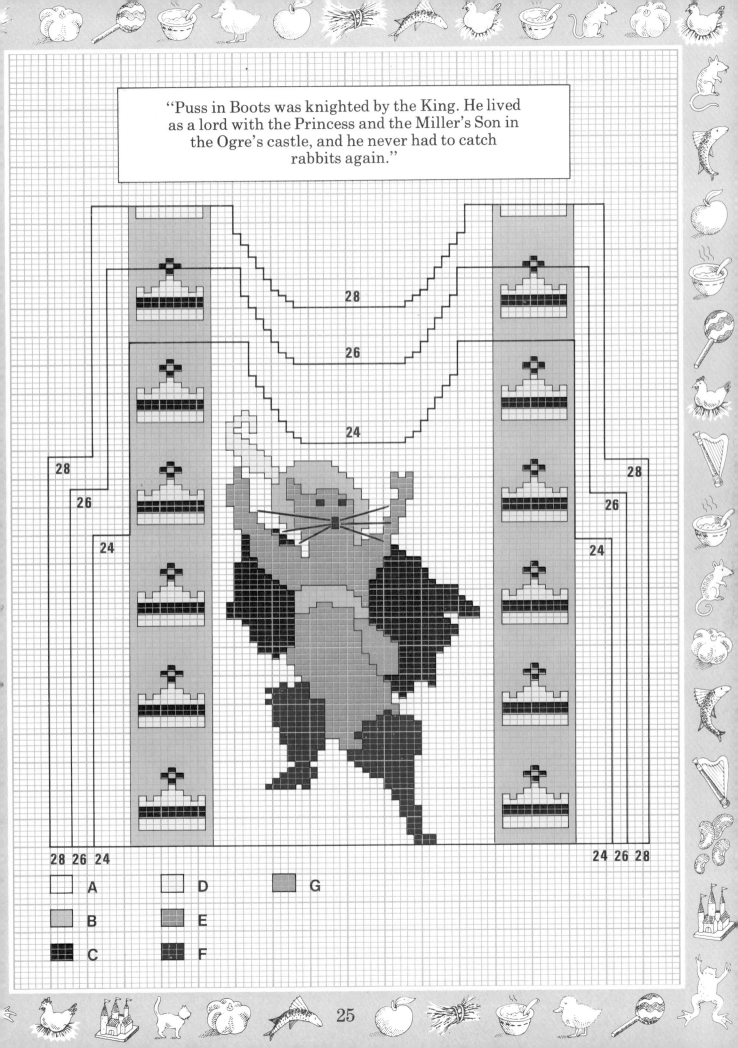

28

26

24

28

26

24

28

26

24

28

26

24

28 26 24

24 26 28

A   D   G

B   E

C   F

Little Red Riding Hood

Based on the traditional folktale as retold by Charles Perrault

There was once a little girl who lived on the edge of a wood with her mother. Because she always wore a bright red hood that her mother had made for her, she was called Little Red Riding Hood.

One day, when her grandmother was not very well, Little Red Riding Hood decided to take her a present of some goodies. As always, her mother warned her to beware of the Wolf who lived in the forest. Little Red Riding Hood promised to keep on the path and not walk through the wood, and to come home before dark. Off she went, taking her basket of apples and cakes. Now, who else should be out walking on that sunny afternoon but the bad old Wolf? With his sharp eyes he spied Little Red Riding Hood, and with his keen nose he could smell the lovely cakes in her basket.

Little Red Riding Hood did not hear the Wolf as her crept up beside her to look in the basket. She jumped in fright when he asked her what she was carrying. She tried to ignore the Wolf but he was very nosy, and finally she told him she had some goodies that she was taking to her grandmother. The Wolf decided to play a trick on Little Red Riding Hood for not giving him any cake. He sped off through the woods towards Grandmother's cottage. He knocked loudly on the door and said in a sweet little voice,

"Grandma, it's Little Red Riding Hood here, with a basket of cakes for your tea."

"Open the door and come in, my dear," said poor Grandma from her bed, and in rushed the Wolf and pushed the old lady into a cupboard, locking her in. Then he took her nightcap and put it on his huge head, and jumped into bed, holding the covers up to his chin.

By the time Little Red Riding Hood reached the cottage all was quiet. She knocked loudly on the door and a gruff voice called out "Come in my dear, the door is open." Inside, the room was all dark, but Little Red Riding Hood could just make out her grandmother.

"What big eyes you've got, Grandma," said Little Red Riding Hood.

"All the better to see you with, my dear," said the Wolf in his gruff voice.

"What big ears you've got, Grandma," said Little Red Riding Hood in surprise, as she came closer to the bed.

"All the better to hear you with, my dear," replied the Wolf.

"And what enormous teeth you've got, Grandma," whispered Little Red Riding Hood in a worried voice, as she stood by the bed.

"All the better to eat you with!" roared the Wolf, and leapt out of bed towards her.

Little Red Riding Hood dropped the basket in fright, and dashed out of the door. All the apples rolled on to the floor behind her, but she did not look round. The Wolf tripped over the apples and fell down with a great crash. Little Red Riding Hood ran screaming back through the woods. Close to home she saw the Woodcutter, who grabbed his shotgun and ran to meet her. Together they returned to the cottage to look for her grandmother. Little Red Riding Hood cried all the way there.

When they arrived, the Wolf was nowhere to be seen. The cottage door was wide open, and there were apples all over the floor. They crept through the door with the gun at the ready in case the Wolf appeared. From the cupboard came the sound of someone calling for help. They ran to open it and found the old lady tied up inside. Little Red Riding Hood and the Woodcutter helped her out and put her back to bed with a large glass of brandy. As for the Wolf, he was so ashamed of missing his tea that he never dared to come out of the forest again.

Little Red Riding Hood

Lower ribbing Light Green

Front of sweater After working the ribbing in Light Green, follow the chart opposite for the picture of Little Red Riding Hood and the Wolf. Remember, purl rows are left to right, and knit rows are right to left. Work the top ribbing in Bright Green.

Back of sweater After working the lower ribbing in Light Green, work the back as shown on the chart, omitting Little Red Riding Hood and the Wolf. Work the top ribbing in Bright Green. Use the small diagram (see right) to knit the trees. Each square shown there represents 10 horizontal stitches and 10 vertical rows.

Sleeves After working the lower ribbing in Light Green, work the entire sleeve in Bright Green, including the top ribbing.

Neckband and Buttonstand Bright Green

Left shoulder opening Bright Green (see p.64 for buttonhole instructions).

Finishing Complete the picture by working a French knot (see p.32) in Lavender Blue for Little Red Riding Hood's eye. Make the Wolf's eye by working a single stitch in Bright Yellow over a Black horizontal Swiss darn ([Duplicate stitch], see p.12). Sew three buttons on to the buttonstand.

Sweater back

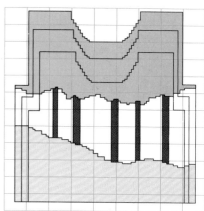

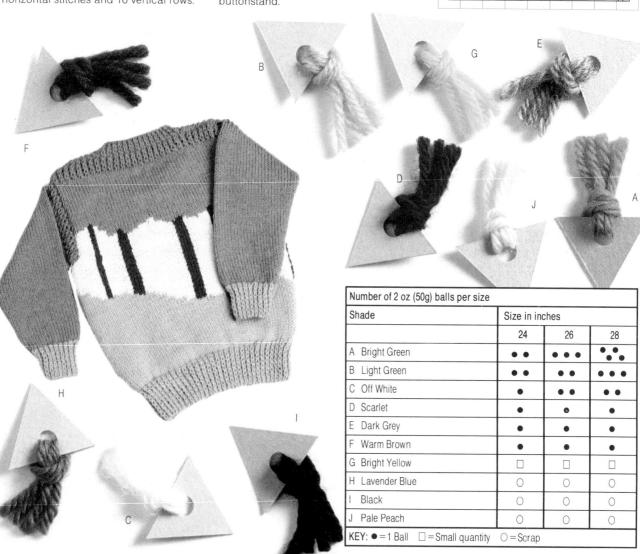

Number of 2 oz (50g) balls per size			
Shade	Size in inches		
	24	26	28
A Bright Green	● ●	● ● ●	● ● ● ● ● ●
B Light Green	● ●	● ●	● ● ●
C Off White	●	● ●	● ●
D Scarlet	●	●	●
E Dark Grey	●	●	●
F Warm Brown	●	●	●
G Bright Yellow	□	□	□
H Lavender Blue	○	○	○
I Black	○	○	○
J Pale Peach	○	○	○
KEY: ● = 1 Ball □ = Small quantity ○ = Scrap			

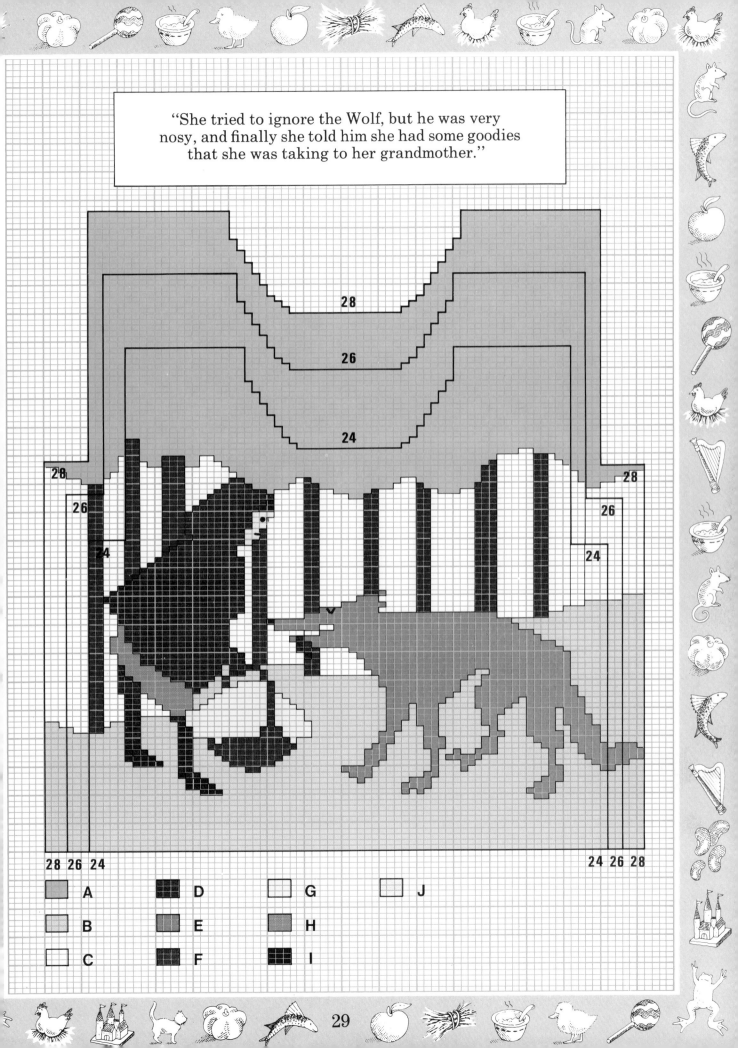

"She tried to ignore the Wolf, but he was very nosy, and finally she told him she had some goodies that she was taking to her grandmother."

Aladdin and The Magic Lamp

Based on the traditional story from The Arabian Nights

A long time ago a boy called Aladdin became very rich, all because a wicked magician travelling through town played a trick on him. The Magician spotted Aladdin playing in the street, and decided to trick him by pretending to be his old uncle returning from abroad. He gave Aladdin a magic ring, and some delicious things to eat, then he took him to many strange and wonderful places. Finally they came to a place in the hills where there was a huge stone door in the rock. After opening the door, the Magician told Aladdin to go down inside the cave and fetch the lamp that he would find there.

Inside, Aladdin found great treasure chests overflowing with gold and silver. A door opened on to a walled garden, and in the wall he found an oil lamp. He took the lamp, and on the way back to the Magician he stopped to pick the fruit on the trees. It was not really fruit at all, but jewels. There were red rubies, green emeralds and yellow sapphires.

When Aladdin reached the cave entrance, he could not get out. The Magician said he would help him, but first Aladdin must give him the lamp. When Aladdin refused, the Magician shouted magic words and the cave door slammed shut. Aladdin cried out for help, but nobody came. So he walked up and down, rubbing his hands to keep warm, and of course, he rubbed the ring too.

Suddenly, there was a thunderous noise, and in front of him appeared an enormous green genie, ready to grant him a wish. Aladdin was so surprised that he was not at all frightened, and quickly asked to be freed from the cave. In a few seconds he was home again, with the old oil lamp in his arms.

Aladdin was hungry and he ate all the bread and cheese that his poor mother had, until there was none left. So the next day they decided to sell the lamp, and started to polish it. All of a sudden, there was a terrible roar, and the Genie of the lamp appeared. Aladdin asked for something to eat, and instantly the Genie gave them enough food to last for a week. The Genie said anything they wanted would be theirs.

Some years passed and Aladdin became a rich man, married to a Princess. The wicked Magician heard he was alive and still had the magic lamp. The Magician was furious. He decided to go and steal the lamp. Off he went, taking a dozen copper lamps with him in a basket. He walked through the city offering new lamps for old, so when the Princess heard him, she foolishly sent a servant to swap the old lamp for a new one.

As soon as the Magician had rubbed the magic lamp, the Genie appeared, and he ordered it to move the palace far away to Africa. When the Sultan looked out of his window, he was amazed to see that the palace had gone, and ordered his soldiers to find Aladdin and chop off his head. Aladdin was out hunting when the soldiers found him, and he was just as astonished as they were. He promised to find the Princess within forty days, and if not, the King could chop off his head.

Aladdin rubbed his magic ring, and the Genie of the ring took him to the Princess, who was overjoyed to see him again. Together they made a plan, and that evening, when the Magician came to visit the Princess, she poisoned his wine and he dropped down dead. Aladdin found the magic lamp. He rubbed it and the Genie appeared to take them home in a flash. When the Sultan looked out of his window the next day, he was surprised to see the palace back where it should be, with his daughter and Aladdin inside. From that day on, Aladdin always kept the magic lamp safe, hidden in a secret place.

Aladdin and The Magic Lamp

Lower ribbing Ochre

Front of sweater After working the ribbing in Ochre, follow the chart opposite for the picture of Aladdin and the Genie. Remember, purl rows are left to right, and knit rows are right to left. Work the top ribbing in Dark Grey.

Back of sweater After working the lower ribbing in Ochre, work the entire back of the sweater in Dark Grey, including the top ribbing.

Sleeves After working the lower ribbing in Ochre, work the entire sleeve in Dark Grey, including the top ribbing.

Neckband and Buttonstand Dark Grey

Left shoulder opening Dark Grey (see p.64 for buttonhole instructions).

Finishing Using Flame Red, work two French knots for the Genie's eyes (see right). Sew three buttons on to the buttonstand.

French knot

Holding the thread down with your left thumb, encircle the thread twice with your needle. Then twist the needle back to the arrow and insert it close to the starting point. Pull the thread through to the back of the knitting.

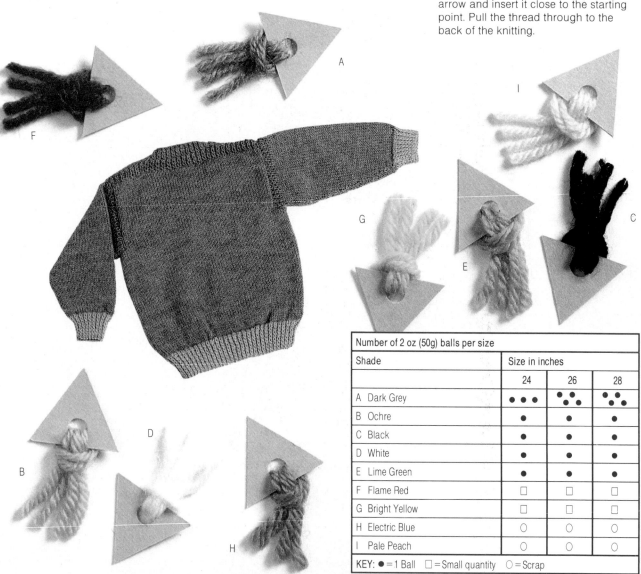

Number of 2 oz (50g) balls per size			
Shade	Size in inches		
	24	26	28
A Dark Grey	● ● ●	● ● ● ●	● ● ● ●
B Ochre	●	●	●
C Black	●	●	●
D White	●	●	●
E Lime Green	●	●	●
F Flame Red	□	□	□
G Bright Yellow	□	□	□
H Electric Blue	○	○	○
I Pale Peach	○	○	○
KEY: ● = 1 Ball □ = Small quantity ○ = Scrap			

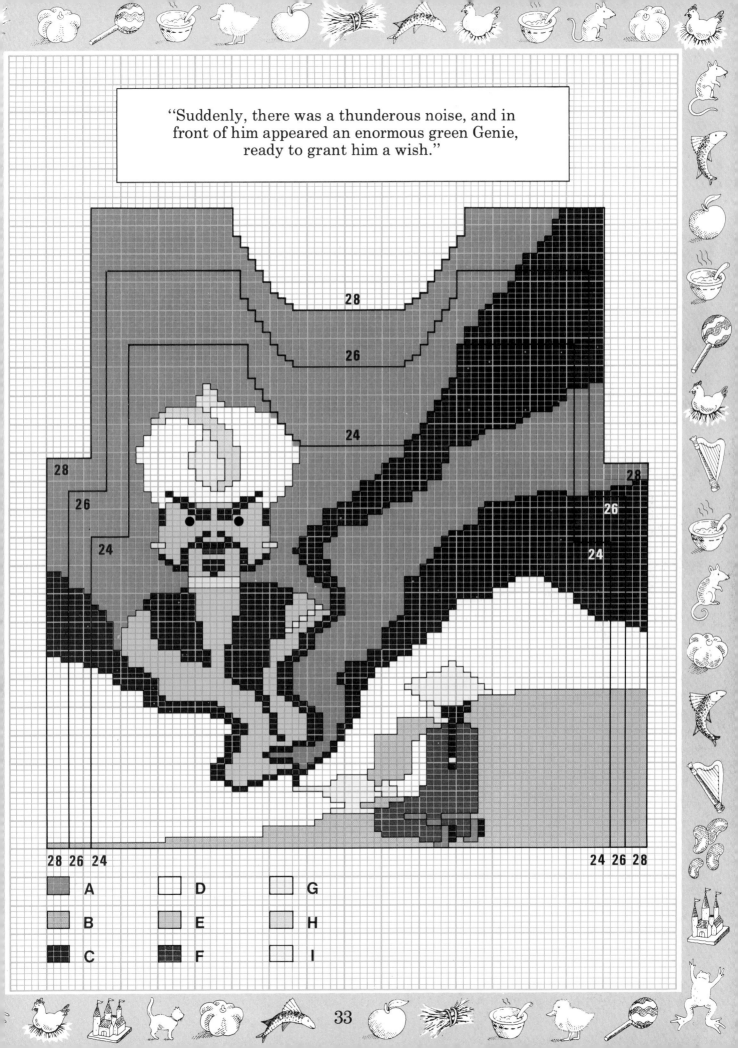

"Suddenly, there was a thunderous noise, and in front of him appeared an enormous green Genie, ready to grant him a wish."

Thumbelina

Based on the fairy tale by Hans Christian Andersen

Once upon a time there was a woman who wanted a little child so much that she went to vist a witch. The Witch gave her some magic barley to plant in a flowerpot, and it grew into a beautiful red tulip. When she kissed it, the flower burst open, and, just as the Witch had promised, there was a tiny girl inside, but only as big as your thumb, so she was named Thumbelina.

One night when Thumbelina was fast asleep, a big, fat toad jumped through the open window, and spied her in her little walnut shell bed. The horrid toad carried her to the muddy stream and sat her on a lily pad, where she could not escape. All the little fishes in the stream felt sorry for Thumbelina, so they untied the lily pad and let it float away from the toad. Down the stream she drifted, until a butterfly came and settled on the lily pad, helping her to sail along more quickly. As they were travelling along, a black cockchafer beetle suddenly swooped down and grabbed Thumbelina, lifting her high into a tree. After a while it dropped her again, and she sat crying on a daisy. All Summer Thumbelina lived alone, eating nectar from the flowers and dew from the grass, and she made herself a little hammock out of grass. The weather slowly grew colder and colder, until it began to snow, and poor little Thumbelina felt very hungry and cold. She wandered through the woods to the house where a field mouse lived and, knocking gently on the door, asked if she could come in.

The Field Mouse was kind, and invited her to stay if she would keep the house tidy. So Thumbelina went to live with the Field Mouse. Their neighbour, the Mole, was rich and clever, and soon fell in love with Thumbelina, hoping that she would marry him one day. Thumbelina did not want to marry a boring old mole and live underground in the dark, where there was no sunshine and no flowers or trees in the garden. One day Thumbelina and the Field Mouse found a swallow lying in the Mole's house. He told them that the bird had died of cold. That night, Thumbelina crept out, taking a bundle of thistledown and a blanket of hay. She wrapped the blanket and the thistledown around the poor bird, and lay down next to it. Suddenly she felt its heart beating. It was not dead at all, but frozen with cold, and the blanket was making it warm again. With Thumbelina's help, the Swallow soon began to feel better, as she gave it food each day. When Spring came, the Swallow was ready to fly away, and Thumbelina was sad to say goodbye, and hoped that her friend would come back one day.

One fine Autumn morning the Field Mouse told Thumbelina to get ready for her wedding. She was very miserable, and went out to look at the sun and the flowers one more time before going to live with the Mole. As she looked up at the blue sky, she saw a beautiful blue bird flying closer and closer, until it swooped down to her, tweeting and calling her name. It was the Swallow, returning to take her to a place where the sun always shines. Thumbelina climbed on to the Swallow's back, and off they flew, high into the sky, over the mountains and seas to a warm and sunny country.

At last they came to a great white palace, and on the ground below lovely flowers everywhere began to open. Inside each one was a little person just like herself only with wings. In one flower was the King, wearing a golden crown, and he asked Thumbelina to be Queen. All the fairy people gave her presents, and little wings so that she could fly.

The next time Spring came to the outside world again, the Swallow said goodbye to Thumbelina, but before he flew across the sea, he promised to come and see her in the Autumn.

Thumbelina

Lower ribbing Baby Blue

Front of sweater After working the ribbing in Baby Blue, follow the chart opposite for the picture of Thumbelina. Remember, purl rows are left to right, and knit rows are right to left. For the top ribbing, continue the cloud shape in White, working the rest in Baby Blue.

Back of sweater Work the lower ribbing in Baby Blue. Continue working in Baby Blue, changing to White as for the front, omitting the Swallow, Thumbelina and the small clouds. For the top ribbing, continue the cloud shape in White, working the rest in Baby Blue.

Sleeves After working the ribbing in White, work the entire sleeve in Baby Blue, including the top ribbing.

Neckband and Buttonstand White

Left shoulder opening Work in white and Baby Blue to match the top ribbing (see p.64 for buttonhole instructions).

Finishing Outline the top of the Swallow's head in Backstitch (see p.8) using Black. Embroider the reins in Pale Lemon using Chainstitch (see right) by carefully working one ribbon from the Swallow's chest to Thumbelina's hand, and another from the back of its head to the front of her dress. Continue to work the Chainstitch behind Thumbelina for the length that you require. Work a French knot in Black for the Swallow's eye (see p.32) (and in Shocking Pink for Thumbelina's mouth). Using Cornflower Blue Swiss darn ([Duplicate stitch] see p.12) her eye. Sew three buttons on to the buttonstand.

Chainstitch

Loop the thread under the tip of your needle, and hold it down with your left thumb while you pick up some of the ground fabric in each stitch. The needle is inserted into the same hole from which it has emerged.

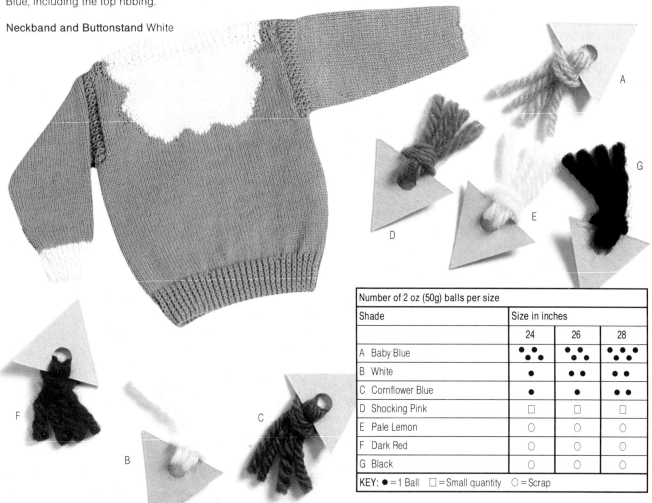

Number of 2 oz (50g) balls per size			
Shade	Size in inches		
	24	26	28
A Baby Blue	●●●	●●●	●●●
B White	●	●●	●●
C Cornflower Blue	●	●	●●
D Shocking Pink	□	□	□
E Pale Lemon	○	○	○
F Dark Red	○	○	○
G Black	○	○	○
KEY: ● =1 Ball □ =Small quantity ○ =Scrap			

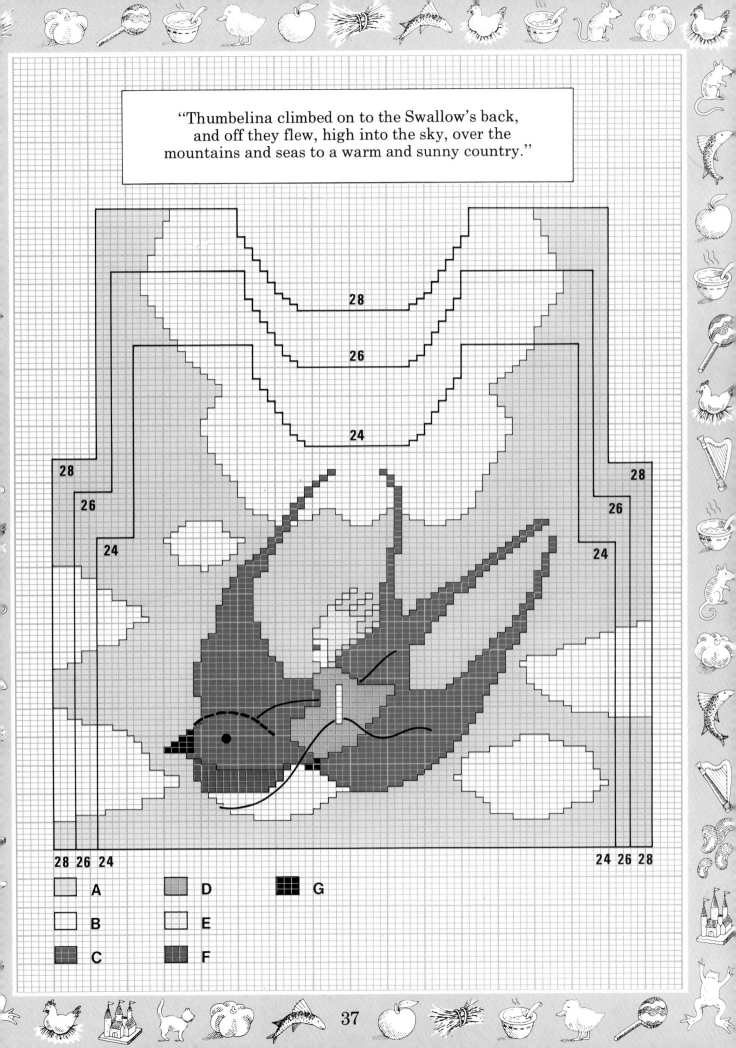

"Thumbelina climbed on to the Swallow's back, and off they flew, high into the sky, over the mountains and seas to a warm and sunny country."

The Ugly Duckling

Based on the fairy tale by Hans Christian Andersen

There was once a duck who had a nestful of little yellow fluffy ducklings and one big grey duckling. The others thought he was scruffy and ugly because he did not look like a duck at all. Every day the mother duck took her ducklings to the pond where they learnt to swim. As she watched them, she always wondered why the biggest duckling was so ugly. All the chickens and ducks in the farmyard laughed at the Ugly Duckling, and some of them even pecked at him because he was different. Sometimes the young girl who fed the chickens shoved him with her foot. Even his brothers and sisters wished that the farm cat would catch him, and his own mother began to wish that he was far away.

So one day he did fly away. Off he went, over the farmyard wall towards the river, where he settled himself in the reeds and watched the wild ducks fly overhead. Even those ducks ignored him, so he thought he must be a very ugly bird indeed.

He spent the rest of the summer paddling forlornly upon the river, with only a few curious fishes and some frogs for company. But they were all busy, and had little time for the duckling, who felt sad as he floated and dived all alone.

Autumn arrived, and all the trees turned golden brown. One evening, as the moon came up, the Ugly Duckling saw a flock of brilliant white birds soaring up into the sky. Over the clouds they flew, shining and bright, with graceful long necks. They spread their wings out and glided across the sky. He was so excited that he turned around and around in the water, flapping his wings and calling loudly. He had never seen such beautiful birds before, and did not know who they were or where they had come from. He called out to the swans but they did not hear him. Sadly he watched them fly away, and his heart felt heavy as he was left all alone once more.

As Winter came, the river froze over, and he could no longer swim in the water. It grew so cold that he found himself stuck fast in the ice, unable to move at all, however hard he struggled. So he lay there, exhausted, lonely and cold. The next morning, a man came along with his dog and saw the poor bird. He broke up the ice with his stick, and carried the duckling home to his wife. All the children wanted to play with him, and he was very frightened by the noise that they made. As they tried to grab him, he fell into the milk pail, splashing milk everywhere, then flew into the butter tub, and finally into the flour barrel, covering everything in flour. The woman screamed at the mess he had made in her kitchen. She rushed to catch him, but he dashed away again, through the open door and out into the thick snow.

All Winter he lived alone by the river, never talking to anyone. When the Spring arrived at last, he tried his wings and found that they were quite strong. So he flew high into the air and over a wall, into a garden full of apple and lilac trees. There was white lilac blossom everywhere. Suddenly three large white birds rose out of the shadows, drifting slowly on the water. He recognised the swans and flew on to the pond towards them. As he saw his reflection below in the water, he realised to his delight that he was no longer an ugly grey bird.

The swans gathered round him, stroking his lovely white feathers with their beaks. Children came to throw bread into the water, admiring the four swans. They ran home to tell their mothers about the new swan, who was the most beautiful one of all. Although he felt shy when everyone said how beautiful he was, he had never been so happy. It was hard to believe that he had ever been an ugly duckling.

The Ugly Duckling

Lower ribbing Dark Green

Front of sweater After working the ribbing in Dark Green, follow the chart opposite for the picture of the Ugly Duckling. Remember, purl rows are left to right, and knit rows are right to left. Work the top ribbing in Lime Green.

Back of sweater Work the lower ribbing in Dark Green, then change to Lime Green for the back of the sweater, including the top ribbing.

Sleeves After working the lower ribbing in Dark Green, work the entire sleeve in Lime Green, including the top ribbing.

Neckband Lime Green

Buttonstand Lime Green

Left shoulder opening Lime Green (see p.64 for buttonhole instructions).

Finishing Once the sweater is completed, work in Satin stitch (see p.16) using Black and White for the Ugly Duckling's eyes. Sew three buttons on to the buttonstand.

Embroidering the eyes

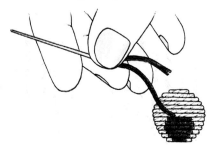

With a scrap of White yarn embroider the larger circle in Satin stitch. Then, using a scrap of Black yarn, work a smaller circle in Satin stitch on top.

Number of 2 oz (50g) balls per size			
Shade	Size in inches		
	24	26	28
A Lime Green	● ●	● ● ●	● ● ●
B Turquoise	●	●	●
C Dove Grey	●	●	●
D Dark Green	●	●	●
E Bright Yellow	●	●	●
F White	●	●	●
G Beige	●	●	●
H Black	●	●	●
I Dark Grey	●	●	●
J Flame Red	○	○	○
KEY: ● = 1 Ball ○ = Scrap			

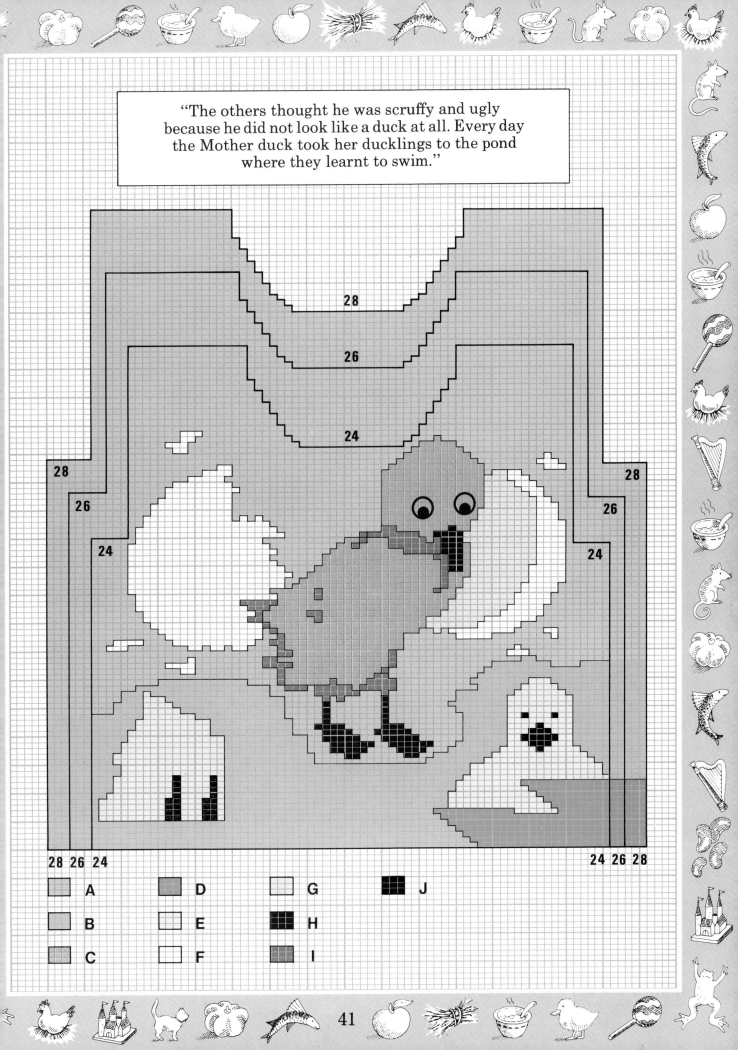

"The others thought he was scruffy and ugly
because he did not look like a duck at all. Every day
the Mother duck took her ducklings to the pond
where they learnt to swim."

The Steadfast Tin Soldier

Based on the fairy tale by Hans Christian Andersen

There was once a toy soldier who lived with a hundred other tin soldiers in a toybox. He was red and blue, and only had one leg, as all the tin had run out, but he managed to stand up on the table just like all the other toys, so he was called the Steadfast Tin Soldier.

One morning, when the children had all the toys out on the floor, the Steadfast Tin Soldier saw the lovely pink Ballerina who lived in the toy castle. She was dancing with one leg tucked up under her skirt, so she looked as if she only had one leg. The Tin Soldier thought she was just like him, and he fell in love with her, even though he had never spoken to her. All the other toys teased him and laughed at him, saying that the Ballerina would never love a tin soldier with only one leg.

The next day, when the window was open and a breeze was blowing in the trees outside, the Steadfast Tin Soldier was blown off the table and out of the window. Down he fell, into the garden, where a bird spotted him lying on the grass, all shiny and bright in his red and blue uniform.

The bird swooped down and picked him up in its beak. As it flew over the garden wall, the bird dropped the Tin Soldier, and down he fell again, into the gutter, where two little boys saw him. They picked him up and wiped the dirt off him. The boys had made a little boat out of white paper, and stood him in it on the water, like the captain of a ship. Away he sailed, with the boys running along beside him, clapping their hands. The paper boat was tossed about on the water, whirling about as the Tin Soldier floated on down the gutter and along the street, bobbing up and down as he went. The boys watched as their little paper boat floated away.

He drifted towards a dark tunnel, and down into the drain, where a great fat water rat popped up and asked to see his passport. But the Tin Soldier did not have a passport, and before the rat could stop him, his little white boat had drifted on down the drain where the rat could not catch up with him.

On and on he went for miles, until at last he reached the big open river, where the little paper boat spun round and round, filling up with water until it collapsed and sank. Out fell the Tin Soldier, down into the deep muddy water, where a silver fish caught sight of him and swallowed him up, even though he did not taste very good. It was not long before a Fisherman came to the river, and he soon caught the big silver fish in his net. The Fisherman took the fish home, and later that day he went to sell it at the market in town. The woman who bought the fish was the Cook who worked in the house where the Tin Soldier lived. When she had washed the fish, she opened it up, where to her surprise, there was the Steadfast Tin Soldier inside.

In a short while he was back with all the other toys in the toybox, where he told them of his adventures in the paper boat. None of the other soldiers believed that he had been carried away in a paper boat and swallowed up by a big fish. The next day, when the Tin Soldier was put on the table, he smiled at the lovely Ballerina. She was smiling at him too, when suddenly one of the children picked him up and threw him into the fire. The boy did not want to play with a one-legged soldier anymore.

The Steadfast Tin Soldier slowly began to melt in the flames. Just at that moment, the door opened and a gust of wind blew the little dancer off the table and into the fire, next to him. For a moment they were together, then she burst into flames and disappeared in a puff of smoke. The next morning all that was left of the Soldier and the Ballerina was a piece of tin shaped like a heart.

The Steadfast Tin Soldier

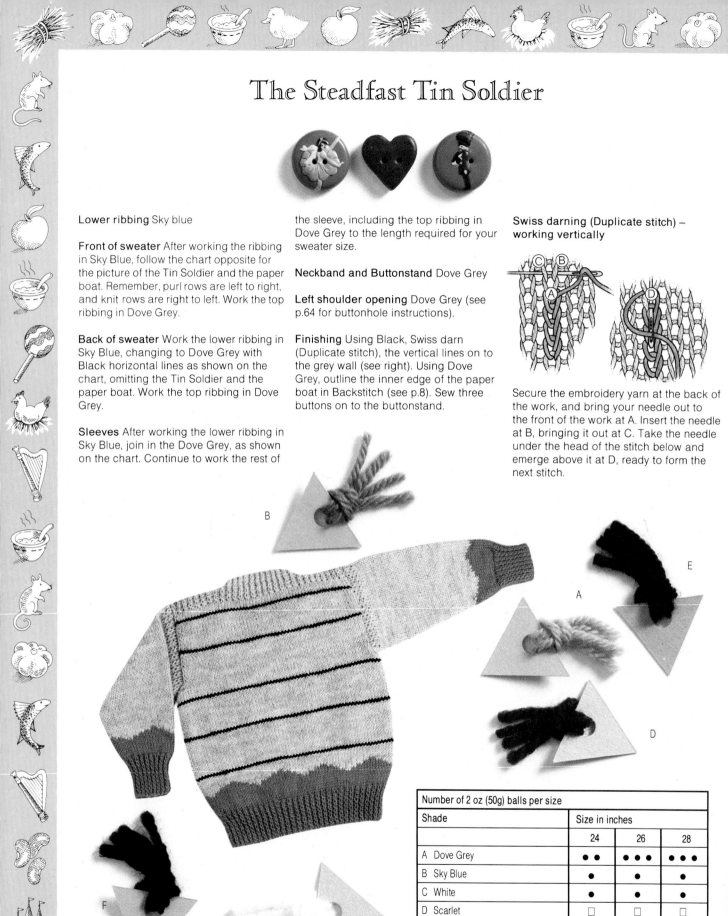

Lower ribbing Sky blue

Front of sweater After working the ribbing in Sky Blue, follow the chart opposite for the picture of the Tin Soldier and the paper boat. Remember, purl rows are left to right, and knit rows are right to left. Work the top ribbing in Dove Grey.

Back of sweater Work the lower ribbing in Sky Blue, changing to Dove Grey with Black horizontal lines as shown on the chart, omitting the Tin Soldier and the paper boat. Work the top ribbing in Dove Grey.

Sleeves After working the lower ribbing in Sky Blue, join in the Dove Grey, as shown on the chart. Continue to work the rest of the sleeve, including the top ribbing in Dove Grey to the length required for your sweater size.

Neckband and Buttonstand Dove Grey

Left shoulder opening Dove Grey (see p.64 for buttonhole instructions).

Finishing Using Black, Swiss darn (Duplicate stitch), the vertical lines on to the grey wall (see right). Using Dove Grey, outline the inner edge of the paper boat in Backstitch (see p.8). Sew three buttons on to the buttonstand.

Swiss darning (Duplicate stitch) – working vertically

Secure the embroidery yarn at the back of the work, and bring your needle out to the front of the work at A. Insert the needle at B, bringing it out at C. Take the needle under the head of the stitch below and emerge above it at D, ready to form the next stitch.

Number of 2 oz (50g) balls per size			
Shade	Size in inches		
	24	26	28
A Dove Grey	● ●	● ● ●	● ● ●
B Sky Blue	●	●	●
C White	●	●	●
D Scarlet	□	□	□
E Royal Blue	□	□	□
F Black	□	□	□
KEY: ● = 1 Ball □ = Small quantity			

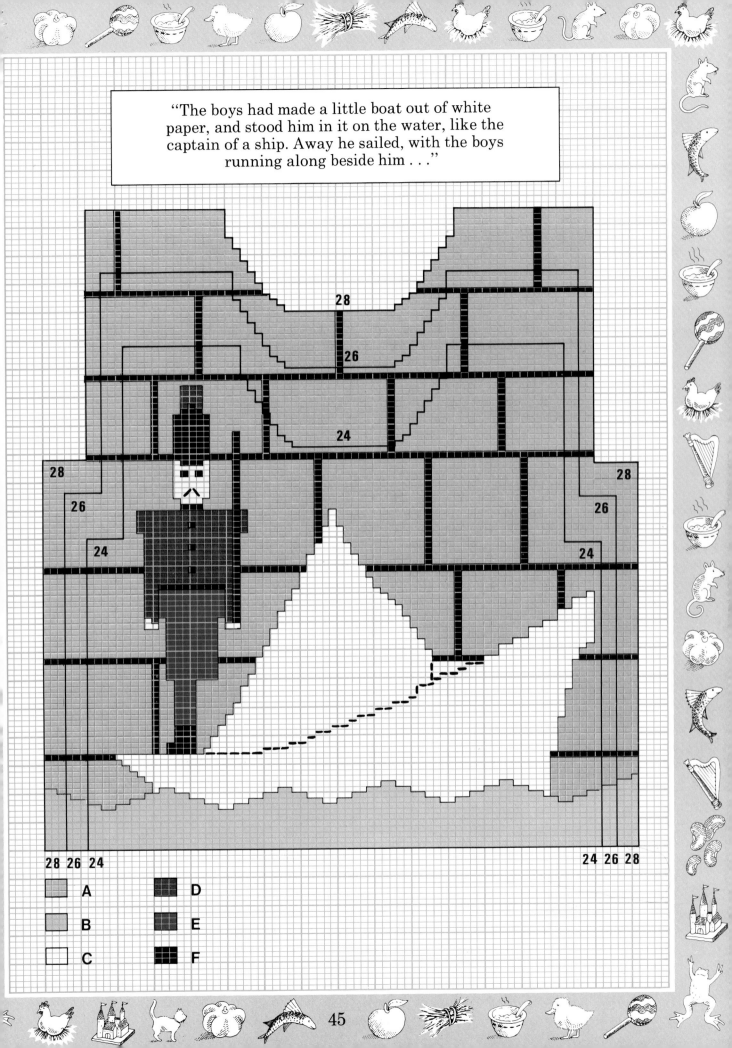

"The boys had made a little boat out of white paper, and stood him in it on the water, like the captain of a ship. Away he sailed, with the boys running along beside him . . ."

Cinderella

Based on the traditional fairy tale as retold by Charles Perrault

Cinderella lived with her stepmother and her two ugly stepsisters, who were horrid to her.

One morning an invitation came for the Ugly Sisters. The King was giving a grand ball. Off they went to the ball, leaving Cinderella at home to tidy the house. She felt very sorry for herself, and wished that she could go too. As she began to cry, her Fairy Godmother appeared.

"You shall go to the ball, my dear," said the kind Fairy, who was the best sort of Godmother. "Go into the garden and bring me the biggest pumpkin that you can find. Then run and fetch me six white mice and bring them here." Cinderella was a good girl, and did as she was told. The Fairy touched the pumpkin with her magic wand, and in an instant it changed into a golden carriage. In a twinkling the mice were turned into beautiful black horses, to pull the carriage along, and before he knew what was happening, the kitchen cat was turned into a coachman.

Cinderella looked down at her ragged dress in dismay. But her Fairy Godmother just smiled, waving her wand through the air. Magic dust blew everywhere, as her skirts billowed out into layers and layers of petticoats, covered with ribbons and lace. Over the top came a deep velvet cloak, with white silk gloves for her hands. On her feet were the prettiest, daintiest shoes of glass. Cinderella looked wonderful.

"Cinderella, there is one thing that you must remember. When the clock strikes twelve, all these fine clothes will disappear, and you will be dressed in rags once more."

When she arrived at the palace, everyone was astonished at the beautiful lady in the golden coach. The King asked who she was, but nobody knew. She was certainly the most elegant person at the ball. The Prince asked Cinderella to dance, which she did so well that he would not dance with anyone else. This made the Ugly Sisters so cross that they both sulked all evening. Suddenly the clock struck twelve. Cinderella jumped up and fled down the steps, out of the garden towards her carriage. As she ran, she slipped and left one shoe on the steps. In the distance she saw her carriage awaiting, but as she came closer, it disappeared, and all that was left was a pumpkin and a fat ginger cat chasing some mice. Cinderella's dress became rags, and she ran home barefoot, carrying her one glass shoe.

The Prince was determined to find Cinderella. He ordered every princess, duchess, countess and lady of the land to come to the palace and try on the shoe. Every day hundreds of women went to the palace in vain, because of course the fairy shoe would only fit Cinderella.

At last the Prince ordered his Messenger to take the shoe to every household in the kingdom. The Messenger went from door to door, and at last he came to the house where Cinderella lived. Both the Ugly Sisters tried to put on the shoe, but their feet were much too large. The Messenger was just about to leave, when he spied Cinderella sweeping the stairs. When he invited her to try on the glass shoe, the Ugly Sisters burst out laughing. But what a surprise they had as she slipped her little foot into the shoe.

"This is the lady who shall marry the Prince," cried the Messenger, who felt very relieved to have found the owner of the shoe at last. Cinderella took the other glass shoe out of her pocket and put it on her foot. She danced around the room in delight, as the Ugly Sisters begged her forgiveness for being so cruel. When she arrived at the palace, the Prince was waiting on the steps, overjoyed to see her again. They were married the next day, and Cinderella never had to sweep the floors again.

Cinderella

Lower ribbing Sugar Pink

Front of sweater After working the ribbing in Sugar Pink, follow the chart opposite for the picture of Cinderella running down the steps. Remember, purl rows are left to right, and knit rows are right to left. Work the top ribbing in Baby Pink.

Back of sweater Work the lower ribbing in Sugar Pink, then work the rest of the back in Baby Pink, including the top ribbing.

Sleeves After working the lower ribbing in Sugar Pink, work the entire sleeve in Baby Pink, including the top ribbing.

Neckband and Buttonstand Baby Pink

Left shoulder opening Baby Pink (see p.64 for buttonhole instructions).

Finishing When the sweater is completed, add pink or silver sequins to Cinderella's ball gown (see right). Work French knots (see p.32) in Ice Blue for her eyes, and Sugar Pink for her mouth. Add hands to the clock with Backstitch (see p.8), and work four small French knots on the quarter hour marks, all in Mink. Sew three buttons on to the buttonstand.

Adding beads and sequins

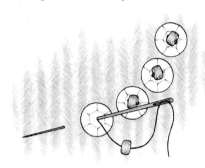

Bring the needle out through the eye of the sequin and thread a small glass bead on to it, then insert the needle back through the eye of the sequin, and pull it tight so that the bead rests firmly over the eye, securing the sequin.

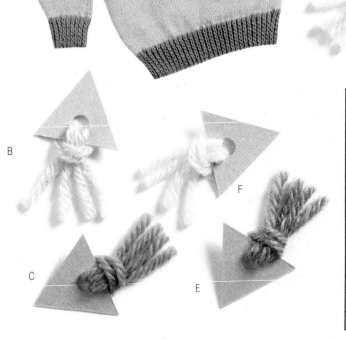

Number of 2 oz (50g) balls per size			
Shade	Size in inches		
	24	26	28
A Baby Pink	●●● ●●	●● ●●	●●● ●●
B Pale Grey	●	●●	●●
C Sugar Pink	●	●●	●●
D White	●	●	●
E Dark Grey	●	●	●
F Pale Lemon	□	□	□
G Mink	□	□	□
H Pale Peach	□	□	□
I Ice Blue	○	○	○
KEY: ● =1 Ball □ =Small quantity ○ =Scrap			

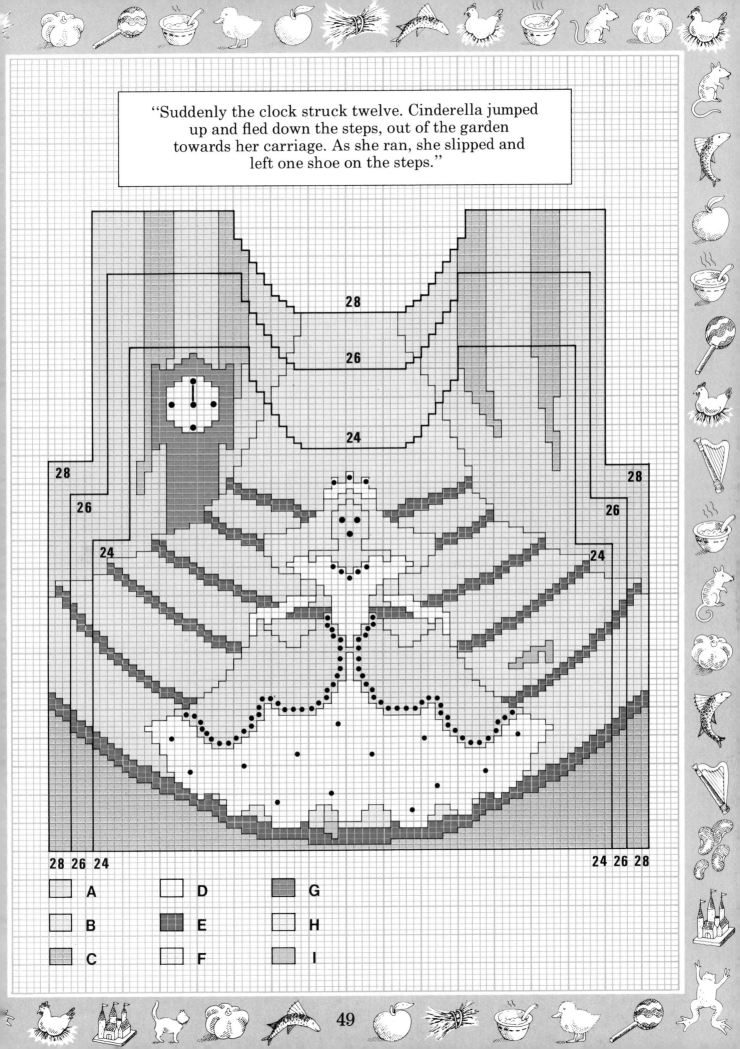

"Suddenly the clock struck twelve. Cinderella jumped
up and fled down the steps, out of the garden
towards her carriage. As she ran, she slipped and
left one shoe on the steps."

Hansel and Gretel

Based on the fairy tale by The Brothers Grimm

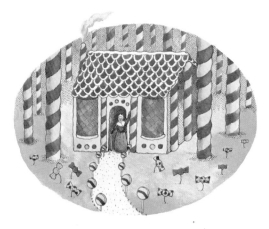

Once upon a time there were two children called Hansel and Gretel who lived near the woods with their father and their stepmother. Their stepmother was always grumbling because they were poor, and one day she told her husband, the Woodcutter to take the children into the woods and leave them there, because there was not enough food left. Hansel heard them talking, so the next day, when their father took them into the woods, he dropped little white pebbles on the ground. Later on that day it was easy to follow the pebbles home, and when their father saw them again he was very happy indeed.

A little while later, the Woodcutter's family ran out of food again, and his wife decided to take the children into the woods and leave them there herself. Hansel and Gretel were each given a piece of bread, and followed their stepmother deep into the woods. As they went deeper into the woods, Hansel dropped little crumbs of white bread on the ground so that they would be able to find their way home, but all the little birds in the woods came to eat the crumbs until there were none left.

Soon it started to get dark, and Hansel and Gretel were left all alone in the woods. They could not see the crumbs on the ground, so they wandered about until morning came. Tired and hungry, Hansel and Gretel spotted a lovely cottage with smoke puffing out of the chimney. It was all made of gingerbread, and its little red roof was decorated with shiny white icing. The windows were made of pink marzipan and there were barley sugar trees and toffees in the garden. It was the most delicious house that they had ever seen, and they rushed to taste it.

As they were munching the gingerbread, the door opened, and out popped a dear old lady. "Come inside children and have some dinner."

The little old lady took the children into her cottage and gave them apple pie and cream, then she tucked them up in bed, where they quickly fell asleep, dreaming of good things to eat.

The next morning the old lady was not sweet anymore. She looked quite horrid, as she was really a bad old witch who liked to eat little children. In a flash, she locked Hansel inside a bird cage, and ordered Gretel to sweep the floors. The Witch kept Hansel in the cage, and every day she fed him on gingerbread to make him fatter so that later she could cook him in the oven. But every time the Witch squeezed his arm to see how fat it was, Hansel stuck out a twig instead of his arm, so the Witch thought he was still too skinny.

One morning the wicked Witch shouted at Gretel to get the big cooking pot ready. Then she told her to get into the oven to see if it was warm enough for baking bread, and little Gretel guessed what was to happen.

"Old Witch, Old Witch, the oven is too small for me to get inside," cried Gretel.

"You silly girl," shouted the Witch, "this is how you get in," and she opened the oven door and stuck her own head inside. At that same moment, Gretel gave her the biggest push that she could, and banged the door shut. Then she let Hansel out of his cage, and they danced for joy.

All the Witch's treasure chests were bursting with gold and jewels, so they filled their pockets with as much as they could carry, and ran through the woods. Soon they saw their house ahead of them, and the Woodcutter and his wife running down the path to them. Hansel and Gretel's parents were overjoyed to see their children again and were very sorry for what they had done. Their stepmother was even happier when she saw the gold, because she knew that they would never be hungry again.

Hansel and Gretel

Lower ribbing Bright Yellow

Front of sweater After working the ribbing in Bright Yellow, follow the chart opposite for the picture of the Witch's cottage. Remember, purl rows are left to right, and knit rows are right to left. Work the right top ribbing in Pale Grey; work the left top ribbing in White.

Back of sweater After working the lower ribbing in Bright Yellow, follow the chart, leaving out the windows and door on the cottage, and the garden. Use the picture of the sweater back on this page as a guide. You will note that the chimney and smoke are on the opposite side of the roof than on the front. You may find it easier

to trace the roof from the chart and reverse it, counting the number of stitches, rather than working directly from the original. Work the right top ribbing in Pale Grey; work the left top ribbing in White.

Sleeves Work the entire sleeve in Bright Yellow, including the top ribbing.

Neckband Pale Grey

Buttonstand White

Left shoulder opening Work in White until it reaches the neckband, and then work in Pale Grey (see p.64 for buttonhole instructions).

Finishing Sew three buttons on to the buttonstand.

Sweater back

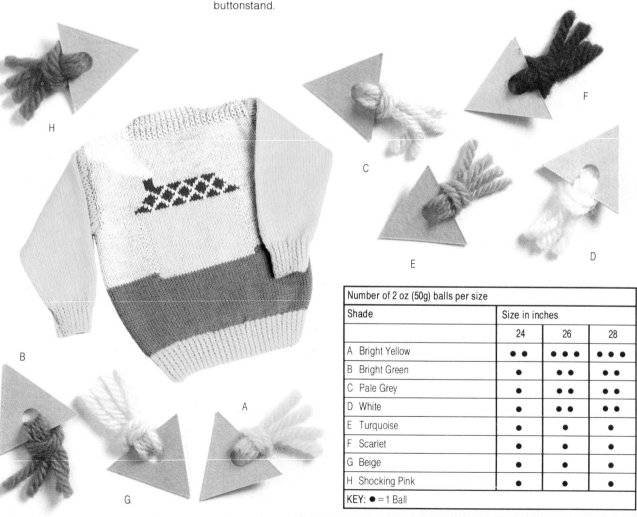

Number of 2 oz (50g) balls per size			
Shade	Size in inches		
	24	26	28
A Bright Yellow	● ●	● ● ●	● ● ●
B Bright Green	●	● ●	● ●
C Pale Grey	●	● ●	● ●
D White	●	● ●	● ●
E Turquoise	●	●	●
F Scarlet	●	●	●
G Beige	●	●	●
H Shocking Pink	●	●	●
KEY: ● = 1 Ball			

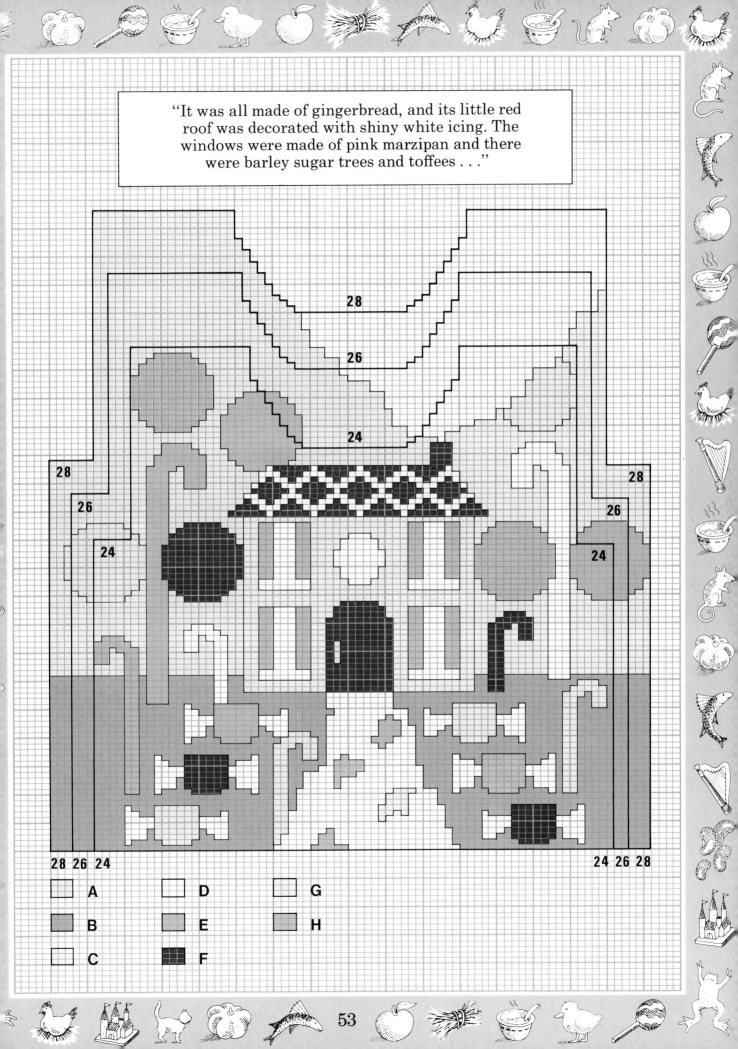

"It was all made of gingerbread, and its little red roof was decorated with shiny white icing. The windows were made of pink marzipan and there were barley sugar trees and toffees . . ."

Equipment

Set out below is some of the knitting equipment that you may need, or find useful, when making the sweaters in the book.

KEY

1 4mm (US No.5) needles These are used to knit the main body of the sweater.

2 3¼mm (US No.3) needles These smaller needles are used for knitting the ribbing on the sweaters.

3 Crochet hook This can be used to join the seams of the garment together securely with a Chainstitch.

4 Wool needle A blunt needle with a large eye is best for making French knots and working other embroidery stitches.

5 Large-eyed needle A thinner needle should be used for sewing the buttons on to the sweater.

6 Stitch holder Use this to hold the divided stitches when knitting the neck.

7 Tape measure You will need a tape measure to check that all your garment measurements are accurate.

8 Marker rings When working complicated designs these can help to separate the different elements.

9 Row counter Put on the blunt end of your knitting needle, this will help you keep track of where you are if your knitting is constantly interrupted.

10 Needle guard To help prevent you from dropping stitches, place this on the pointed end of your knitting needle.

11 Thread and yarn holder When knitting designs with many colours in a row, these will keep the ends from getting tangled.

12 Knitting notions Manufactured safety eyes or fabric motifs can give the sweaters a more individual character.

13 Scissors Small, sharp scissors can be kept handy in your knitting bag.

14 Pins Pins with brightly-coloured heads that are not easily lost should be used when joining the knitted pieces.

15 Buttons A wide range of pretty and colourful buttons are available to finish off your particular fairy tale sweater.

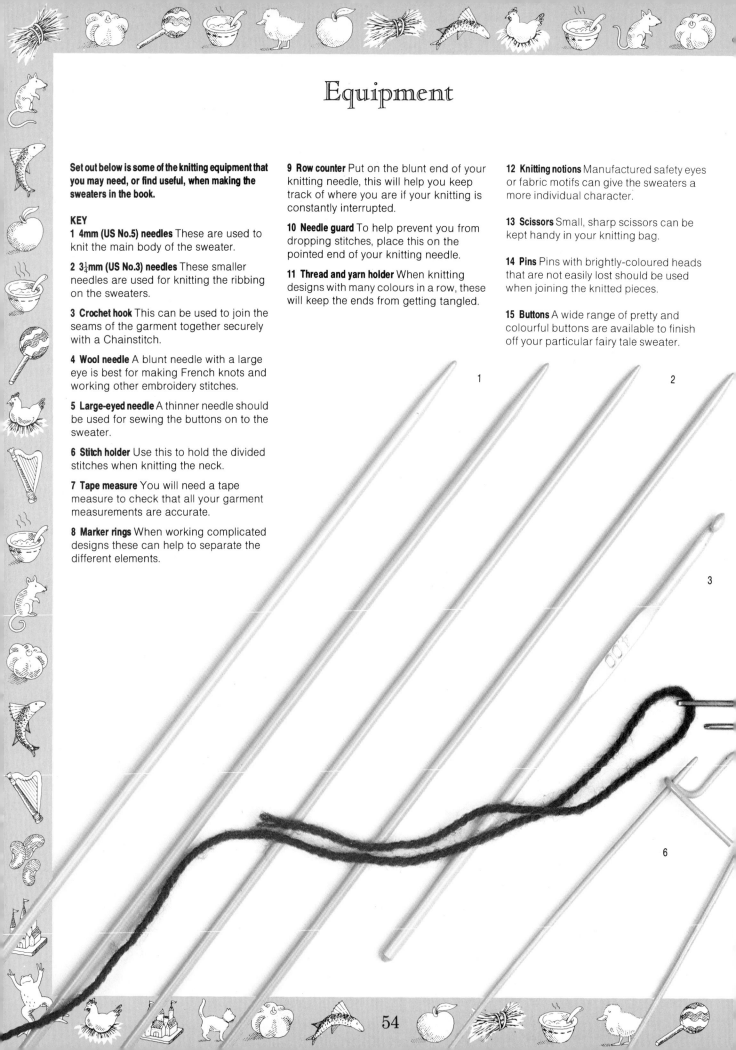

WORKING FROM THE PATTERN CHARTS

On the charts accompanying every sweater design, each square represents one stitch. The charts are always read from the bottom of the chart upwards, and from right to left on the first and all odd-numbered rows. Therefore, the bottom right-hand corner indicates the first stitch. You must always knit all the odd-numbered rows and purl all the even-numbered rows.

The charts are coloured to reflect the yarns used on the sweaters.

Underneath each chart is an alphabetical key to the particular shades used. These colours are described generally, and do not reflect any one manufacturer's range.

The black dots and dotted lines on the pattern charts indicate where to place French knots and other embroidery stitches that are described in detail with the sweater instructions.

Start Purl rows ▶

Start Knit rows ▲

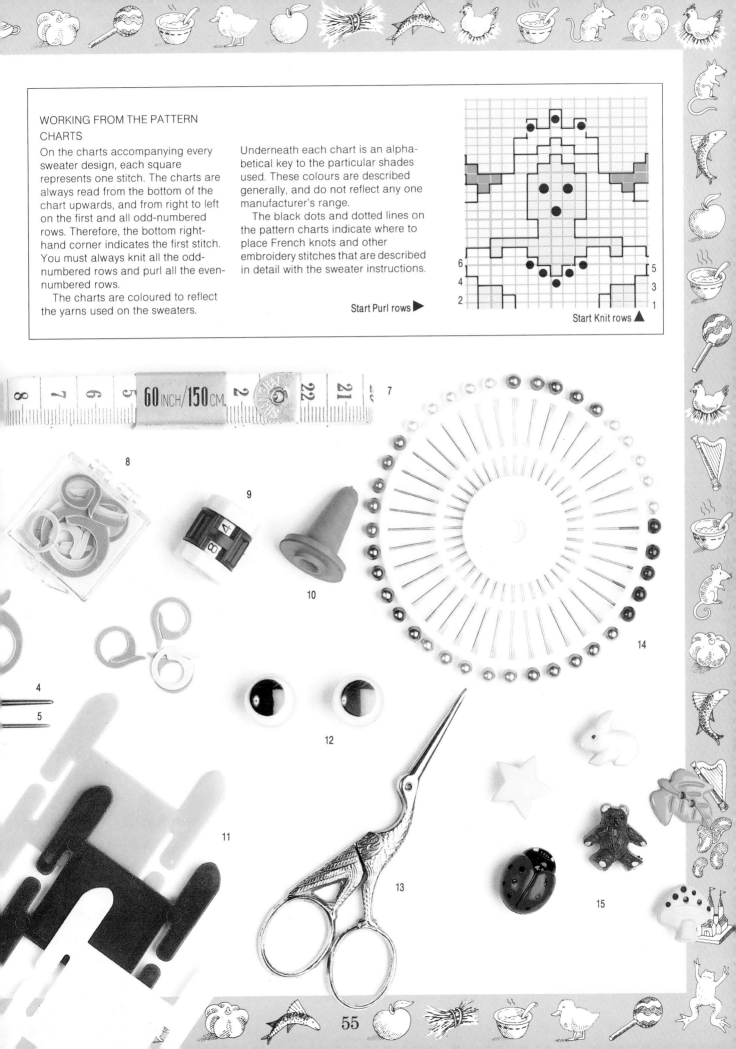

Working with Yarn

Each of the colourful sweaters has been knitted in Emu Superwash Double Knitting yarn, as shown here. These yarns are machine washable 100% pure new wool, with a choice of 74 shades. Each shade is accompanied by a code number which you will need to quote when ordering EMU yarn. If you have difficulty in purchasing any of the EMU shades, they are all obtainable through the distributors listed on p. 64. You can, of course, use other yarn than the one we have chosen. It is only necessary that your yarn knits to a tension of 30 rows and 23 stitches to a 4 inch (10cm) square on 4mm needles in stocking (stockinette) stitch. When knitting for children, some knitters prefer yarns that contain some synthetic fibres. Emu Supermatch has excellent washing and non-allergic qualities. When washing pure wool, gentle handling is most important. Hand wash or machine wash at a maximum of 40°C, then rinse in cool water. Do not wring, but give the sweater a short spin, or roll it in a dry towel and gently squeeze, then dry flat. Alternatively, dry clean.

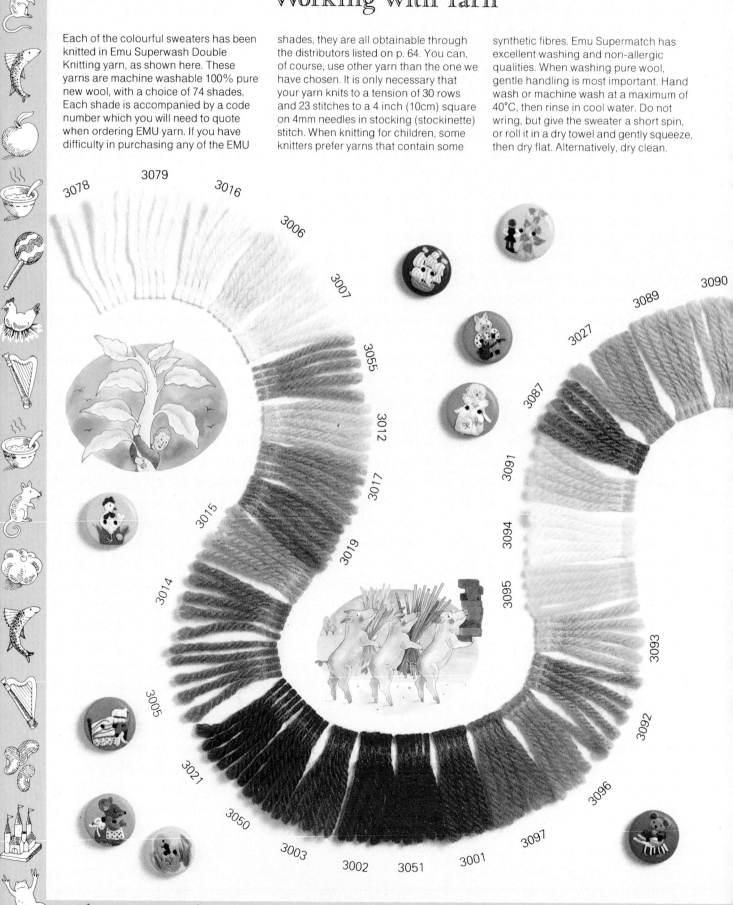

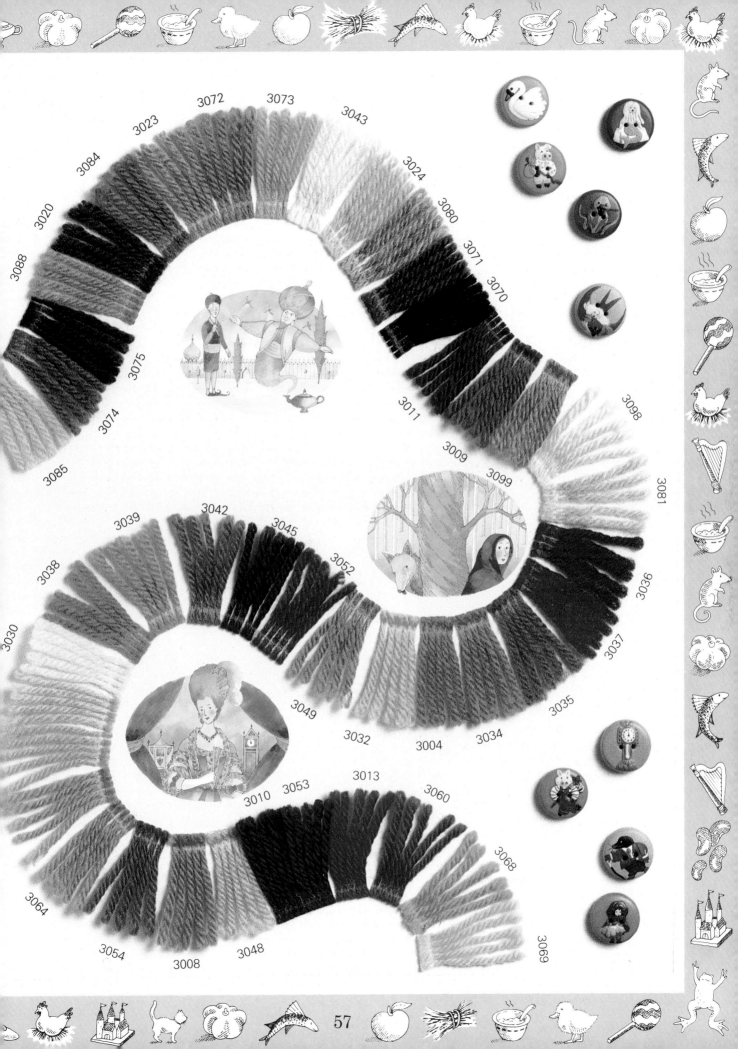

3072
3073
3023
3043
3084
3024
3020
3080
3088
3071
3070
3075
3011
3074
3009
3085
3099
3098
3081
3042
3045
3039
3052
3038
3036
3030
3037
3035
3049
3004 3034
3032
3010 3053
3013
3060
3064
3068
3054
3008 3048
3069

Beginning to Knit

When you begin to work on a pattern placing the first row of stitches on the needle is known as 'casting on'. All further rows are worked into these initial loops. This can be done on one or two needles and the method may be specified in the pattern.

SINGLE CAST ON

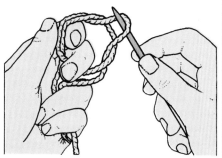

1 Wrap your yarn around two fingers twice and pull a loop through the twisted yarn with a knitting needle.

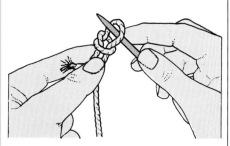

2 Pull both ends of the yarn to tighten. This produces a slip loop.

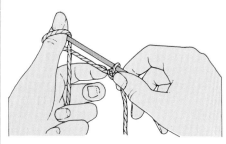

3 With the slip loop on your right-hand needle wrap the working end of the yarn around your left thumb and hold it in the palm of your hand. Put the needle through the yarn behind the thumb.

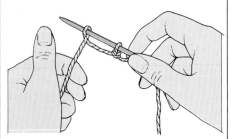

4 Lift the yarn and slide the new 'stitch' towards the slip loop. Tighten the working end to secure the stitch until you have the required number.

TWO-NEEDLE CAST ON

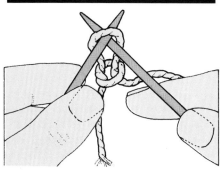

1 With the slip loop on your left-hand needle, insert your right-hand needle through the loop from front to back.

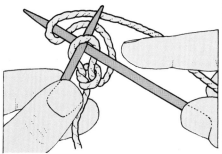

2 Bring the yarn under and over your right-hand needle.

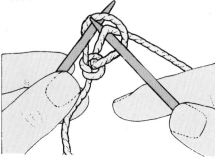

3 Draw up the yarn through the slip loop to make a stitch.

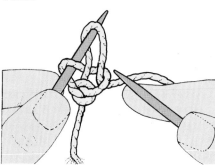

4 Place the stitch on your left-hand needle. Continue to make stitches drawing the yarn through the last stitch on your left-hand needle.

CASTING (BINDING) OFF

When you end a piece of knitting you must secure all the stitches you have finished by "casting off". This should be done on a knit row but you can employ the same technique on a purl row: the stitches, whether knit or purl, should be made loosely. When casting off rib, you must use both knit and purl.

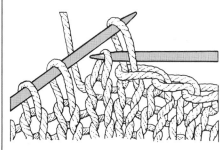

IN A KNIT ROW

1 Knit the first two stitches and insert the tip of your left-hand needle through the first stitch.

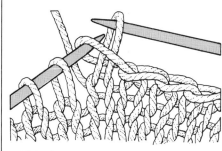

2 Lift the first stitch over the second stitch and discard it. Knit the next stitch and continue to lift the first stitch over the second stitch to the end of the row. Be careful not to knit too tightly. For the last stitch, cut your yarn, slip the end through the stitch and pull the yarn tight to fasten off securely.

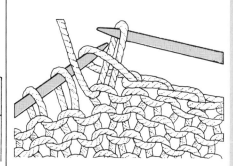

IN A PURL ROW

Purl the first two (and all subsequent) stitches and continue as for knit stitch above.

Basic Stitches

Knit stitch and purl stitch are the two basic knitting stitches. Either one worked continuously in rows forms Garter stitch pattern and worked alternately forms Stocking (Stockinette) stitch pattern.

KNIT STITCH (K)

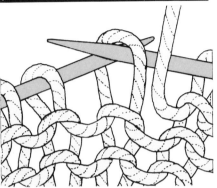

1 With the yarn at the back, insert your right-hand needle from front to back into the first stitch on your left-hand needle.

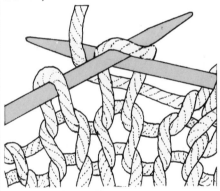

2 Bring your working yarn under and over the point of your right-hand needle.

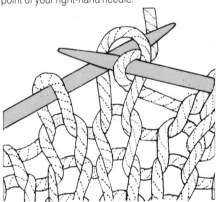

3 Draw a loop through and slide the first stitch off your left-hand needle while the new stitch is retained on your right-hand needle. Continue in this way to the end of the row.

4 To knit the next row, turn the work around so that the back is facing you and the worked stitches are held on the needle in your left hand. Proceed to make stitches as above, with the initially empty needle held in your right hand.

PURL STITCH (P)

1 With the yarn at the front, insert your right-hand needle from back to front into the first stitch on your left-hand needle.

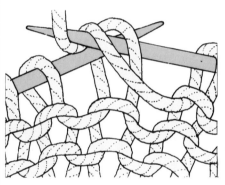

2 Bring your working yarn over and around the point of your right-hand needle.

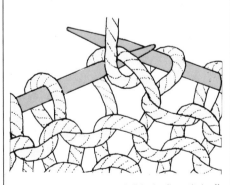

3 Draw a loop through and slide the first stitch off your left-hand needle while the new stitch is retained on your right-hand needle. Continue in this way to the end of the row.

4 To purl the next row, turn the work around so that the back is facing you and the worked stitches are held on the needle in your left hand. Proceed to makes stitches as above, with the initially empty needle held in your right hand.

STOCKING (STOCKINETTE) STITCH (st st)

Knitting the first and every odd row and purling the second and every even row produces Stocking (Stockinette) stitch.

RIBBING

A combination of knit and purl stitches, usually one or two knit stitches and then one or two purl stitches, in the same row is known as ribbing. Ribbing is used on sleeve and body edges to form a neat, stretchable finish. It is usually worked on smaller needles than the main body of the garment.

TENSION (STITCH GAUGE)

Before starting to make any garment you must make a tension sample in order to measure stitch gauge. You should do this in order to check your individual control of the yarn against the pattern, so the measurements are the same as in the pattern.

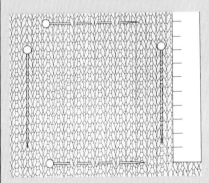

The stitch gauge, or tension, is always given at the beginning of a pattern. It is written as the number of stitches, and the number of rows in a particular pattern, e.g. stocking stitch, to a specified size, such as 10cm, using the yarn and needles called for in the pattern. An example is 32 sts and 32 rows to 10cm over st st pattern on 4mm needles.

A variation in tension within a garment will result in an uneven appearance. By knitting the required number of stitches and rows, your sample will reveal whether the yarn and needles you are using will make up into the size and shape you require. When working your tension sample, you must take into account the pattern and the method of carrying yarns across the back of the work (see p. 61).

Correcting Mistakes

DROPPED STITCHES

Occasionally, a stitch may fall off your needle, in which case correct it by following one of the techniques described below. Dropped stitches are often the result of leaving work in the middle of a row.

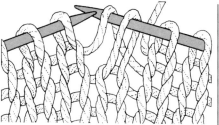 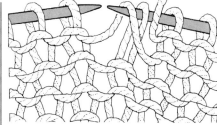

PICKING UP A DROPPED KNIT STITCH

1 Pick up both the stitch and strand on your right-hand needle, inserting the needle from front to back.

PICKING UP A DROPPED PURL STITCH

1 Pick up both the stitch and strand on your right-hand needle, inserting the needle from back to front.

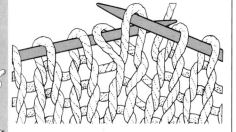 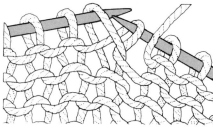

2 Insert your left-hand needle through the stitch only, from back to front. With your right-hand needle only, pull the strand through the stitch to make the extra stitch. (Drop the stitch from your left-hand needle.)

2 Insert your left-hand needle through the stitch only, from front to back. With your right-hand needle only, pull the strand through the stitch to make the extra stitch. (Drop the stitch from your left-hand needle.)

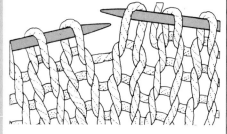 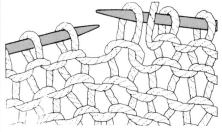

3 Transfer the re-formed stitch back to your left-hand needle, so that it untwists and faces the correct way. It is now ready for knitting again.

3 Transfer the re-formed stitch back to your left-hand needle, so that it untwists and faces the correct way. It is now ready for purling again.

UNPICKING MISTAKES

Holding the stitch on your right-hand needle insert your left-hand needle into the row below and undo the stitch. Transfer the stitch back to your right-hand needle and repeat undoing until the error has been reached. Correct stitch as for a ladder, see right.

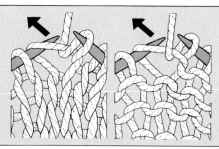

LADDERS

If a dropped stitch is left, it can unravel down the work and form a "ladder". The easiest way to correct this is to use a crochet hook to pick up the stitches in pattern, although you can try to correct it with your needles.

If you make a mistake in your knitting, you may have to "unpick" a stitch, which can result in a ladder. Pick up one dropped stitch at a time, securing any others with a safety pin to prevent further unraveling.

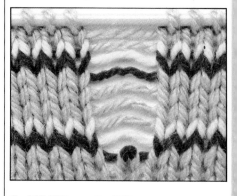

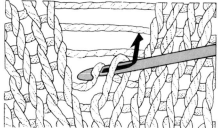

CORRECTING A KNIT LADDER

Insert a crochet hook through the front of the dropped stitch. Hook up one strand and pull it through the stitch to form a new stitch one row up. Continue in this way to the top of the ladder then continue in pattern.

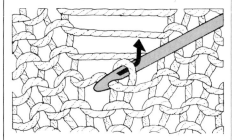

CORRECTING A PURL LADDER

Insert a crochet hook through the back of the dropped stitch. Hook up one strand and pull it through the stitch to form a new stitch one row up. Continue to re-insert hook to make stitches until you reach the top of the ladder, then continue in pattern.

Working with Colours

When knitting with more than one colour, you will need to adopt various techniques to keep the back of the work neat and to prevent holes appearing. The three basic methods of working are: stranding, weaving and crossing.

ADDING YARN AT THE BEGINNING OF A ROW

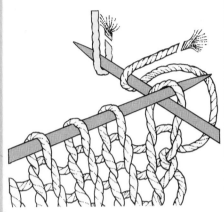

1 Insert your right-hand needle through the first stitch on your left-hand needle and wrap the old yarn, and then the new yarn over it. Knit (or purl) the stitch using both yarns.

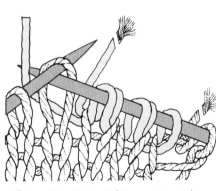

2 Leaving the old yarn at the back, knit (or purl) the next two stitches using the double length of the new yarn.

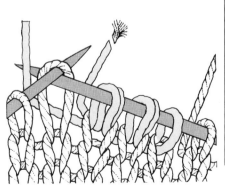

3 Discard the short end of the new yarn and continue to knit as usual. On the following row, treat the three double stitches as single stitches.

ADDING A YARN IN THE MIDDLE OF A ROW

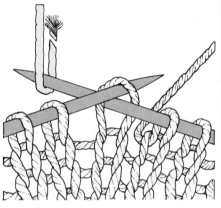

1 Insert your right-hand needle through the first stitch on your left-hand needle. Wrap the new yarn over, and knit (or purl) the stitch with the new yarn. Leave the old yarn at the back of the work.

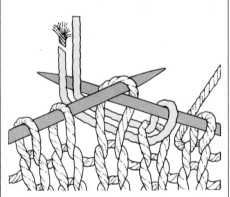

2 Knit (or purl) the next two stitches using the double length of the new yarn.

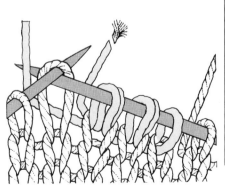

3 Discard the short end of the new yarn and continue to knit as usual. On the following row, treat the two double stitches as single stitches.

STRANDING YARN

Use this method for working narrow stripes, and other patterns requiring only two colours in a row. Strand yarn over a maximum of five stitches only.

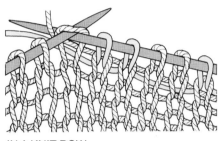

IN A KNIT ROW

With both yarns at the back of the work, knit the required number of stitches with yarn A (in this case two), and then drop it to the back. Pick up yarn B and knit the required number of stitches and then drop it to the back. Both yarns should be stranded loosely along the back of the work.

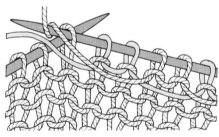

IN A PURL ROW

With both yarns at the front of the work, purl the required number of stitches with yarn A (in this case two), and then drop it. Pick up yarn B and purl the required number of stitches and then drop it. Both yarns should be stranded loosely along the front (side facing you).

Working with Colours

WEAVING YARN

This method should be used when you are working large pattern repeats, for patterns requiring three or more colours, and when yarn has to be carried over more than five stitches.

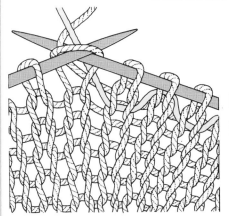

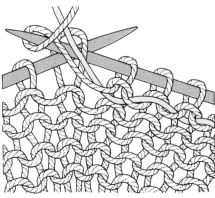

IN A KNIT ROW

1 Hold yarn A in your right hand and yarn B in your left hand to the back of the work.

IN A PURL ROW

1 Hold yarn A in your right hand and yarn B in your left hand to the front of the work.

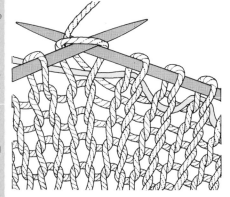

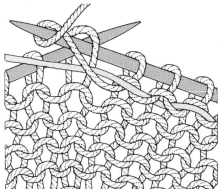

2 Knit one stitch with yarn A and, at the same time, bring yarn B below yarn A. When yarn B is being used, weave yarn A as above.

2 Purl one stitch with yarn A but this time bring yarn B below yarn A. When yarn B is being used, weave yarn A as above.

CHECKING YOUR TECHNIQUE

WEAVING

If you have worked weaving correctly, the yarns will cross evenly and remain at the same depth. A "smocking" effect means that you have pulled the yarns too tightly. It is better for the yarns to be woven too loosely than too tightly.

STRANDING

If you have worked stranding correctly, the yarns will be running evenly across the back of the work at the same tension as the knitting.

Puckering indicates that you have pulled the yarns too tightly.

CROSSING COLOURS

Use this method for working small blocks of colour. When crossing colours each colour is kept as a separate ball or on a bobbin and is not taken across the work. Rather, the yarns are crossed at the join. Follow the instructions below for vertical colour patterns as well, but cross the colours on every row.

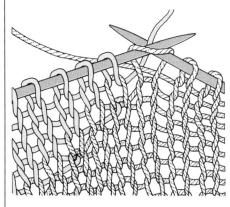

IN A KNIT ROW FOR A DIAGONAL STRIPE TO THE RIGHT

Cross yarn A in front of yarn B and drop it to the back. Knit the first stitch on your left-hand needle using yarn B. On the return row the yarns will automatically loop together.

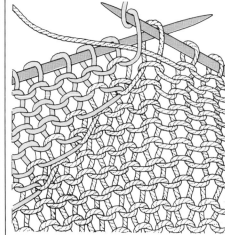

IN A PURL ROW FOR A DIAGONAL STRIPE TO THE LEFT

Pick up yarn B in front of yarn A and use it to purl the next stitch on your left-hand needle. On the return row, the yarns will automatically loop together.

Other Techniques

SEAMS

Your pattern will usually set out the order of seaming: normally the shoulder seams are joined first if you have to pick up stitches to make the neck band. There is a choice of two methods, the edge-to-edge seam and the backstitch seam.

An edge-to-edge seam is useful on lightweight knits because it is almost invisible and forms no ridge.

A backstitch seam is stronger and firmer and is suitable for all garments but it forms a ridge.

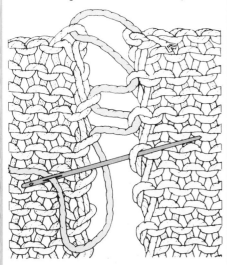

EDGE-TO-EDGE SEAM

Place the pieces to be joined edge-to-edge with the "heads" of the knit stitches locking together. Match the pattern pieces carefully row for row and stitch for stitch. Using the main yarn, sew into the head of each stitch alternately.

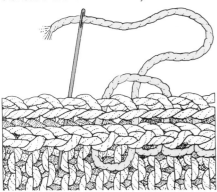

BACKSTITCH SEAM

Place the pieces to be joined together with their right sides facing. Carefully match pattern to pattern, row to row and stitch to stitch. Sew along the seam using backstitch sewing into the center of each stitch to correspond with the stitch on the opposite piece. Sew ¼in (6mm) in from the edge of the knitting.

INCREASING

INCREASE 1 (Inc 1)

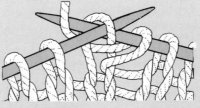

IN A KNIT ROW

Knit into the front of the stitch in the usual way. Without discarding the stitch on your left-hand needle, knit into the back of it, making two stitches.

IN A PURL ROW

Purl into the front of the stitch in the usual way. Without discarding the stitch on your left-hand needle, purl into the back of it, making two stitches.

DECREASING

KNITTING TWO STITCHES TOGETHER (K2 tog)

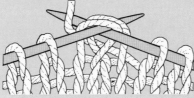

IN A KNIT ROW (K2 tog)

Insert your right-hand needle through the front of the first two stitches on your left-hand needle. Knit them together as a single stitch.

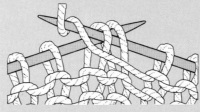

IN A PURL ROW (P2 tog)

Insert your right-hand needle through the front of the first two stitches on your left-hand needle. Purl them together as a single stitch.

FINISHING TECHNIQUES

Before pattern pieces are joined up, they are usually blocked and pressed to ensure a good fit. It's always a good idea to check the yarn band for any special instructions. The pieces are blocked when dry and are pressed with a cloth.

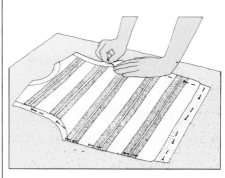

BLOCKING

Garment pieces need blocking, or putting into shape before they can be joined up. Cover a table with a folded blanket and a sheet. Using rustless pins, "block" the pieces wrong-side out to the correct measurements. Be careful not to stretch or distort the fabric and make sure that all the rows run in straight lines.

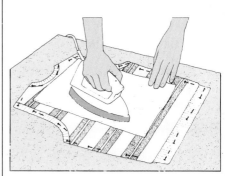

PRESSING

After blocking, the garment pieces are usually pressed in position. Use a warm iron and a cloth on wool. Lay the iron on the fabric and lift it up, do not move it over the surface. Do not remove any of the pins until the work has cooled and dried completely.

Ribbing should be lightly stretched and pinned before ironing. Use a heavy cloth and remove the pins in order to adjust the fabric while it is still warm.

Basic Sweater Pattern

These are finished garment measurements. The child's actual measurements should be smaller.

MEASUREMENTS
Chest size
24/26/28in (60,65,70cm)

Length to shoulder
14½/16/17½in (37/40/44cm)

Sleeve seam
10½/12/13in (27/30/33cm)

Abbreviations
k = knit; p = purl; patt = pattern; st(s) = stitch(es); st st = stocking stitch (stockinette stitch).

Tension (Stitch Gauge)
23 sts and 30 rows measure 10cm over pattern on 4mm (US No.5) needles.

MATERIALS
Yarn
Emu Superwash (or Supermatch) DK, knitting worsted or any other standard double knitting wool, quantity as stated on your chosen pattern chart page.

Needles
Suggested sizes
1 pair 3¼mm needles (UK No.10, US No.3)
1 pair 4mm needles (UK No.8, US No.5)

Notions
3 buttons

FRONT
** With 3¼mm (US No.3) needles cast on 66/72/78 sts. Work 16/16/16 rows in k1, p1 rib, following colour instructions given with individual sweater design. Always go into the back of every knit stitch to give a twisted effect. Increase 4/3/3 sts evenly across last row to make 70/75/81 sts. Change to 4mm (US No.5) needles and st st. Work straight in pattern from chosen chart until front measures 9/10/11in (23/25/28cm) from cast-on edge.

Shape armholes
Cast off 5/5/6 sts at beginning of next 2 rows to make 60/65/69 sts. ** Continue straight, following chart until armhole measures 2½/3/3½in (6/7.5/9cm).

Divide for neck
Next row: Pattern 23/25/27 sts, cast off next 14/15/15 sts loosely, patt 23/25/27 sts. Continue on last set of sts, decreasing 1 st at neck edge on next 2/2/3 rows then 1 st at this edge on following 5/5/5 alternate rows – 16/18/19 sts remain. Work straight, following chart

until armhole measures 4¾/5¼/5¾in (12/13/14cm), ending with wrong-side row. Then work 5/5/5 rows twisted rib. Cast off right across in rib. Work left side of neck on remaining stitches, reversing shapings. Work until armhole measures 4½/5/5½in (11.5/12.5/13.5cm). Finish as for right side.

BACK
Work as for front from ** to ** following instructions for ribbing and rest of back given with the individual design. Continue straight until armhole measures 4¾/5¼/5¾in (12/13/14cm) from start of armhole shaping, ending with wrong-side row. Then work 5/5/5 rows k1, p1 twisted rib. Cast off right across loosely in rib.

SLEEVES
With 3¼mm (US No.3) needles cast on 39/40/41 sts. Work 16/18/18 rows twisted rib in colours as directed on individual design, increasing 4/4/4 sts evenly across last row to make 43, 44, 45 sts. Change to 4mm (US No.5) needles and colours as directed, and shape sides by increasing 1 st at each end of 3rd and every following 5th/5th/5th row until there are 63/68/73 sts. Work straight until sleeve measures 10/11/12¼in (25/28/30cm) from cast-on edge, ending with wrong-side row. Then work 5/5/5 rows twisted rib and cast off right across.

NECKBAND
Join right shoulder seam. With 3¼mm (US No.3) needles begin at left shoulder and pick up one stitch for each row of knitting all around neck, using colours as directed on individual design. Work 5/5/5 rows twisted rib. Cast off in rib.

Left shoulder opening and buttonholes
With 3¼mm (US No.3) needles pick up and knit 22/23/24 sts across left front shoulder and up side of neck ribbing, using colours as directed on individual design. Work 1 row in twisted rib. Make 3 buttonholes in next row thus: Rib 3/4/4 (cast-off 2, rib 5/5/5) twice, cast-off 2, rib 3/3/4.
Next row: Work in rib, casting on 2 over those cast-off. Work a further 2 rows rib; cast-off.

Buttonstand
With 3¼mm (US No.3) needles pick up and knit 22/23/24 sts down side of neck rib and along back of left shoulder in colour as directed on individual design. Work 5 rows twisted rib; cast off in rib.

FINISHING
Lap buttonhole band of shoulder opening over buttonstand at the back. Catch down double fabric at armhole edge. Join right shoulder seam. Pin cast-off edge of sleeve top to form a neat right-angle at cast-off sts of armhole on back and front. Join with backstitch, then join rest of seams. Sew on buttons.

USEFUL INFORMATION
Distributors of EMU Yarn

U.K.	Consumer Services EMU Wools Ltd Leeds Road Bradford West Yorkshire BD10 9TE Tel: (0274) 614031
U.S.A.	The Plymouth Yarn Co Inc P.O. Box 28 500 Lafayette Street Bristol PA 19007 Tel: (215) 788 0459
South Africa	Brasch Hobby P.O. Box 6405 Johannesburg 2000 Tel: (683) 7237
Canada	S R Kertzer Ltd 105A Winges Road Woodbridge Ontario L4L 6C2 Tel: (416) 856 3447
Australia	Karingal Vic/Tas Pty Ltd 6 Macro Court Rowville Victoria 3187 Tel: (03) 764 1433

Buttons
The Fairytale buttons are obtainable from Duttons for Buttons, 15 Lowther Arcade, Harrogate HG1 1RZ, England.
Tel: (0423) 502092 (mail orders – please enclose s.a.e.).
For general enquiries only, contact Baboushka Ltd., 39 Bowerham Road, Lancaster, Lancs LA1 4AE, England.

ACKNOWLEDGEMENTS
Many thanks to the following people for all their help: Sally Hibbard for design assistance, Gilly Newman for the colour technique illustrations, Pat White for administrative assistance and Christine Kingdom at Emu Wools Ltd.

Correcting Mistakes

DROPPED STITCHES

Occasionally, a stitch may fall off your needle, in which case correct it by following one of the techniques described below. Dropped stitches are often the result of leaving work in the middle of a row.

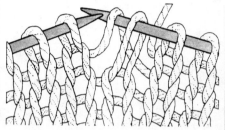

PICKING UP A DROPPED KNIT STITCH

1 Pick up both the stitch and strand on your right-hand needle, inserting the needle from front to back.

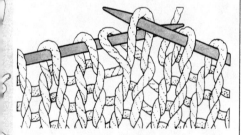

2 Insert your left-hand needle through the stitch only, from back to front. With your right-hand needle only, pull the strand through the stitch to make the extra stitch. (Drop the stitch from your left-hand needle.)

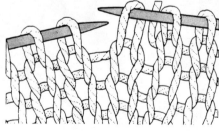

3 Transfer the re-formed stitch back to your left-hand needle, so that it untwists and faces the correct way. It is now ready for knitting again.

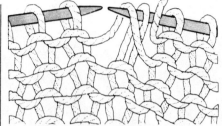

PICKING UP A DROPPED PURL STITCH

1 Pick up both the stitch and strand on your right-hand needle, inserting the needle from back to front.

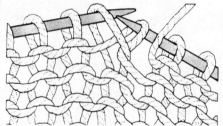

2 Insert your left-hand needle through the stitch only, from front to back. With your right-hand needle only, pull the strand through the stitch to make the extra stitch. (Drop the stitch from your left-hand needle.)

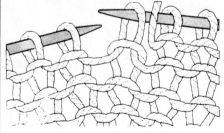

3 Transfer the re-formed stitch back to your left-hand needle, so that it untwists and faces the correct way. It is now ready for purling again.

UNPICKING MISTAKES

Holding the stitch on your right-hand needle insert your left-hand needle into the row below and undo the stitch. Transfer the stitch back to your right-hand needle and repeat undoing until the error has been reached. Correct stitch as for a ladder, see right.

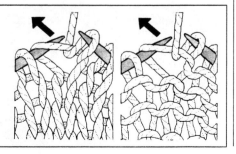

LADDERS

If a dropped stitch is left, it can unravel down the work and form a "ladder". The easiest way to correct this is to use a crochet hook to pick up the stitches in pattern, although you can try to correct it with your needles.

If you make a mistake in your knitting, you may have to "unpick" a stitch, which can result in a ladder. Pick up one dropped stitch at a time, securing any others with a safety pin to prevent further unraveling.

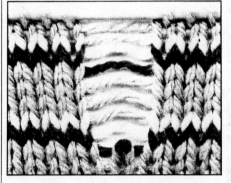

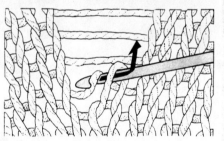

CORRECTING A KNIT LADDER

Insert a crochet hook through the front of the dropped stitch. Hook up one strand and pull it through the stitch to form a new stitch one row up. Continue in this way to the top of the ladder then continue in pattern.

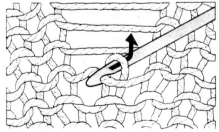

CORRECTING A PURL LADDER

Insert a crochet hook through the back of the dropped stitch. Hook up one strand and pull it through the stitch to form a new stitch one row up. Continue to re-insert hook to make stitches until you reach the top of the ladder, then continue in pattern.

Correcting Mistakes

DROPPED STITCHES

Occasionally, a stitch may fall off your needle, in which case correct it by following one of the techniques described below. Dropped stitches are often the result of leaving work in the middle of a row.

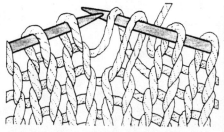

PICKING UP A DROPPED KNIT STITCH

1 Pick up both the stitch and strand on your right-hand needle, inserting the needle from front to back.

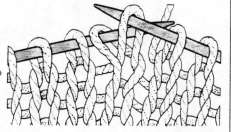

2 Insert your left-hand needle through the stitch only, from back to front. With your right-hand needle only, pull the strand through the stitch to make the extra stitch. (Drop the stitch from your left-hand needle.)

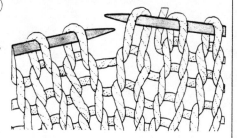

3 Transfer the re-formed stitch back to your left-hand needle, so that it untwists and faces the correct way. It is now ready for knitting again.

PICKING UP A DROPPED PURL STITCH

1 Pick up both the stitch and strand on your right-hand needle, inserting the needle from back to front.

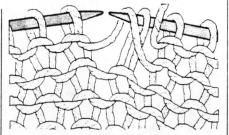

2 Insert your left-hand needle through the stitch only, from front to back. With your right-hand needle only, pull the strand through the stitch to make the extra stitch. (Drop the stitch from your left-hand needle.)

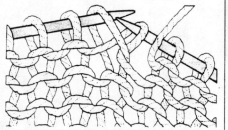

3 Transfer the re-formed stitch back to your left-hand needle, so that it untwists and faces the correct way. It is now ready for purling again.

UNPICKING MISTAKES

Holding the stitch on your right-hand needle insert your left-hand needle into the row below and undo the stitch. Transfer the stitch back to your right-hand needle and repeat undoing until the error has been reached. Correct stitch as for a ladder, see right.

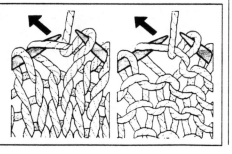

LADDERS

If a dropped stitch is left, it can unravel down the work and form a "ladder". The easiest way to correct this is to use a crochet hook to pick up the stitches in pattern, although you can try to correct it with your needles.

If you make a mistake in your knitting, you may have to "unpick" a stitch, which can result in a ladder. Pick up one dropped stitch at a time, securing any others with a safety pin to prevent further unraveling.

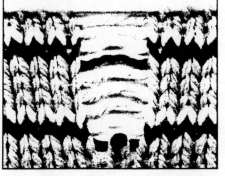

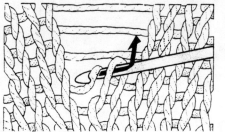

CORRECTING A KNIT LADDER

Insert a crochet hook through the front of the dropped stitch. Hook up one strand and pull it through the stitch to form a new stitch one row up. Continue in this way to the top of the ladder then continue in pattern.

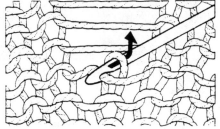

CORRECTING A PURL LADDER

Insert a crochet hook through the back of the dropped stitch. Hook up one strand and pull it through the stitch to form a new stitch one row up. Continue to re-insert hook to make stitches until you reach the top of the ladder, then continue in pattern.

Correcting Mistakes

DROPPED STITCHES

Occasionally, a stitch may fall off your needle, in which case correct it by following one of the techniques described below. Dropped stitches are often the result of leaving work in the middle of a row.

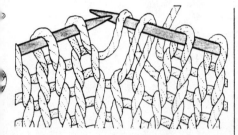

PICKING UP A DROPPED KNIT STITCH

1 Pick up both the stitch and strand on your right-hand needle, inserting the needle from front to back.

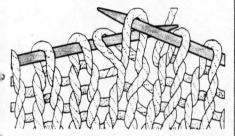

2 Insert your left-hand needle through the stitch only, from back to front. With your right-hand needle only, pull the strand through the stitch to make the extra stitch. (Drop the stitch from your left-hand needle.)

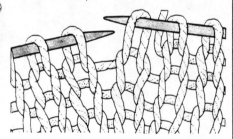

3 Transfer the re-formed stitch back to your left-hand needle, so that it untwists and faces the correct way. It is now ready for knitting again.

PICKING UP A DROPPED PURL STITCH

1 Pick up both the stitch and strand on your right-hand needle, inserting the needle from back to front.

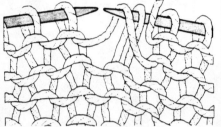

2 Insert your left-hand needle through the stitch only, from front to back. With your right-hand needle only, pull the strand through the stitch to make the extra stitch. (Drop the stitch from your left-hand needle.)

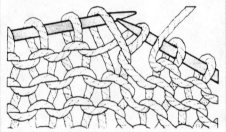

3 Transfer the re-formed stitch back to your left-hand needle, so that it untwists and faces the correct way. It is now ready for purling again.

UNPICKING MISTAKES

Holding the stitch on your right-hand needle insert your left-hand needle into the row below and undo the stitch. Transfer the stitch back to your right-hand needle and repeat undoing until the error has been reached. Correct stitch as for a ladder, see right.

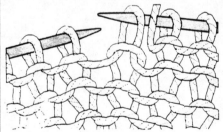

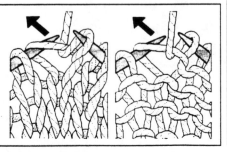

LADDERS

If a dropped stitch is left, it can unravel down the work and form a "ladder". The easiest way to correct this is to use a crochet hook to pick up the stitches in pattern, although you can try to correct it with your needles.

If you make a mistake in your knitting, you may have to "unpick" a stitch, which can result in a ladder. Pick up one dropped stitch at a time, securing any others with a safety pin to prevent further unraveling.

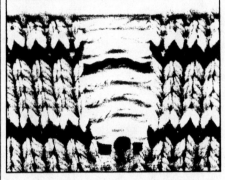

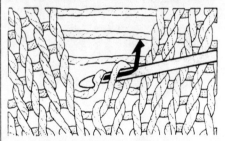

CORRECTING A KNIT LADDER

Insert a crochet hook through the front of the dropped stitch. Hook up one strand and pull it through the stitch to form a new stitch one row up. Continue in this way to the top of the ladder then continue in pattern.

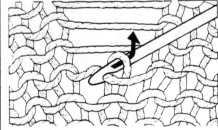

CORRECTING A PURL LADDER

Insert a crochet hook through the back of the dropped stitch. Hook up one strand and pull it through the stitch to form a new stitch one row up. Continue to re-insert hook to make stitches until you reach the top of the ladder, then continue in pattern.

DROPPED STITCHES

Occasionally, a stitch may fall off your needle, in which case correct it by following one of the techniques described below. Dropped stitches are often the result of leaving work in the middle of a row.

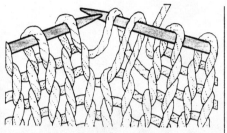

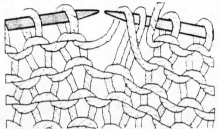

PICKING UP A DROPPED KNIT STITCH

1 Pick up both the stitch and strand on your right-hand needle, inserting the needle from front to back.

PICKING UP A DROPPED PURL STITCH

1 Pick up both the stitch and strand on your right-hand needle, inserting the needle from back to front.

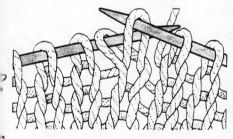

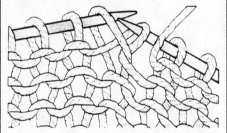

2 Insert your left-hand needle through the stitch only, from back to front. With your right-hand needle only, pull the strand through the stitch to make the extra stitch. (Drop the stitch from your left-hand needle.)

2 Insert your left-hand needle through the stitch only, from front to back. With your right-hand needle only, pull the strand through the stitch to make the extra stitch. (Drop the stitch from your left-hand needle.)

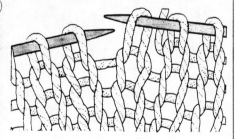

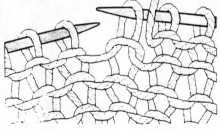

3 Transfer the re-formed stitch back to your left-hand needle, so that it untwists and faces the correct way. It is now ready for knitting again.

3 Transfer the re-formed stitch back to your left-hand needle, so that it untwists and faces the correct way. It is now ready for purling again.

UNPICKING MISTAKES

Holding the stitch on your right-hand needle insert your left-hand needle into the row below and undo the stitch. Transfer the stitch back to your right-hand needle and repeat undoing until the error has been reached. Correct stitch as for a ladder, see right.

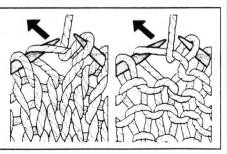

LADDERS

If a dropped stitch is left, it can unravel down the work and form a "ladder". The easiest way to correct this is to use a crochet hook to pick up the stitches in pattern, although you can try to correct it with your needles.

If you make a mistake in your knitting, you may have to "unpick" a stitch, which can result in a ladder. Pick up one dropped stitch at a time, securing any others with a safety pin to prevent further unraveling.

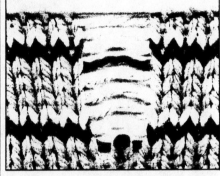

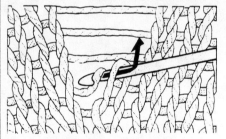

CORRECTING A KNIT LADDER

Insert a crochet hook through the front of the dropped stitch. Hook up one strand and pull it through the stitch to form a new stitch one row up. Continue in this way to the top of the ladder then continue in pattern.

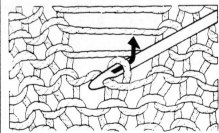

CORRECTING A PURL LADDER

Insert a crochet hook through the back of the dropped stitch. Hook up one strand and pull it through the stitch to form a new stitch one row up. Continue to re-insert hook to make stitches until you reach the top of the ladder, then continue in pattern.

Basic Stitches

Knit stitch and purl stitch are the two basic knitting stitches. Either one worked continuously in rows forms Garter stitch pattern and worked alternately forms Stocking (Stockinette) stitch pattern.

KNIT STITCH (K)

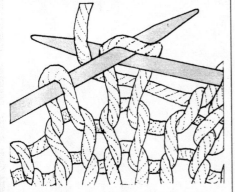

1 With the yarn at the back, insert your right-hand needle from front to back into the first stitch on your left-hand needle.

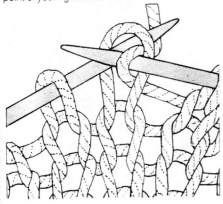

2 Bring your working yarn under and over the point of your right-hand needle.

3 Draw a loop through and slide the first stitch off your left-hand needle while the new stitch is retained on your right-hand needle. Continue in this way to the end of the row.

4 To knit the next row, turn the work around so that the back is facing you and the worked stitches are held on the needle in your left hand. Proceed to make stitches as above, with the initially empty needle held in your right hand.

PURL STITCH (P)

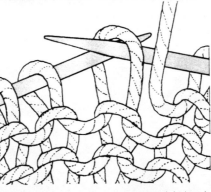

1 With the yarn at the front, insert your right-hand needle from back to front into the first stitch on your left-hand needle.

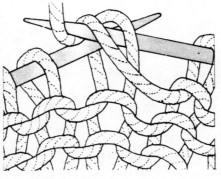

2 Bring your working yarn over and around the point of your right-hand needle.

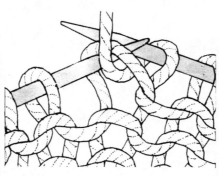

3 Draw a loop through and slide the first stitch off your left-hand needle while the new stitch is retained on your right-hand needle. Continue in this way to the end of the row.

4 To purl the next row, turn the work around so that the back is facing you and the worked stitches are held on the needle in your left hand. Proceed to makes stitches as above, with the initially empty needle held in your right hand.

STOCKING (STOCKINETTE) STITCH (st st)

Knitting the first and every odd row and purling the second and every even row produces Stocking (Stockinette) stitch.

RIBBING

A combination of knit and purl stitches, usually one or two knit stitches and then one or two purl stitches, in the same row is known as ribbing. Ribbing is used on sleeve and body edges to form a neat, stretchable finish. It is usually worked on smaller needles than the main body of the garment.

TENSION (STITCH GAUGE)

Before starting to make any garment you must make a tension sample in order to measure stitch gauge. You should do this in order to check your individual control of the yarn against the pattern, so the measurements are the same as in the pattern.

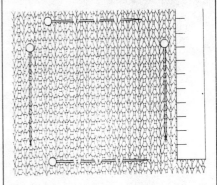

The stitch gauge, or tension, is always given at the beginning of a pattern. It is written as the number of stitches, and the number of rows in a particular pattern, e.g. stocking stitch, to a specified size, such as 10cm, using the yarn and needles called for in the pattern. An example is 32 sts and 32 rows to 10cm over st st pattern on 4mm needles.

A variation in tension within a garment will result in an uneven appearance. By knitting the required number of stitches and rows, your sample will reveal whether the yarn and needles you are using will make up into the size and shape you require. When working your tension sample, you must take into account the pattern and the method of carrying yarns across the back of the work (see p. 61).

Other Techniques

SEAMS

Your pattern will usually set out the order of seaming: normally the shoulder seams are joined first if you have to pick up stitches to make the neck band. There is a choice of two methods, the edge-to-edge seam and the backstitch seam.

An edge-to-edge seam is useful on lightweight knits because it is almost invisible and forms no ridge.

A backstitch seam is stronger and firmer and is suitable for all garments but it forms a ridge.

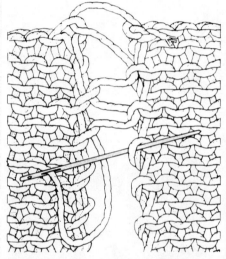

EDGE-TO-EDGE SEAM

Place the pieces to be joined edge-to-edge with the "heads" of the knit stitches locking together. Match the pattern pieces carefully row for row and stitch for stitch. Using the main yarn, sew into the head of each stitch alternately.

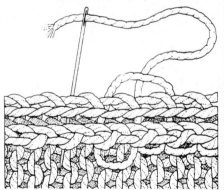

BACKSTITCH SEAM

Place the pieces to be joined together with their right sides facing. Carefully match pattern to pattern, row to row and stitch to stitch. Sew along the seam using backstitch sewing into the center of each stitch to correspond with the stitch on the opposite piece. Sew ¼in (6mm) in from the edge of the knitting.

INCREASING

INCREASE 1 (Inc 1)

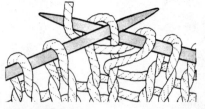

IN A KNIT ROW

Knit into the front of the stitch in the usual way. Without discarding the stitch on your left-hand needle, knit into the back of it, making two stitches.

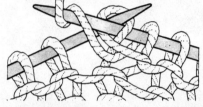

IN A PURL ROW

Purl into the front of the stitch in the usual way. Without discarding the stitch on your left-hand needle, purl into the back of it, making two stitches.

DECREASING

KNITTING TWO STITCHES TOGETHER (K2 tog)

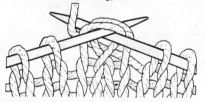

IN A KNIT ROW (K2 tog)

Insert your right-hand needle through the front of the first two stitches on your left-hand needle. Knit them together as a single stitch.

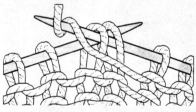

IN A PURL ROW (P2 tog)

Insert your right-hand needle through the front of the first two stitches on your left-hand needle. Purl them together as a single stitch.

FINISHING TECHNIQUES

Before pattern pieces are joined up, they are usually blocked and pressed to ensure a good fit. It's always a good idea to check the yarn band for any special instructions. The pieces are blocked when dry and are pressed with a cloth.

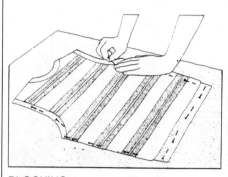

BLOCKING

Garment pieces need blocking, or putting into shape before they can be joined up. Cover a table with a folded blanket and a sheet. Using rustless pins, "block" the pieces wrong-side out to the correct measurements. Be careful not to stretch or distort the fabric and make sure that all the rows run in straight lines.

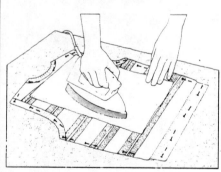

PRESSING

After blocking, the garment pieces are usually pressed in position. Use a warm iron and a cloth on wool. Lay the iron on the fabric and lift it up, do not move it over the surface. Do not remove any of the pins until the work has cooled and dried completely.

Ribbing should be lightly stretched and pinned before ironing. Use a heavy cloth and remove the pins in order to adjust the fabric while it is still warm.

Beginning to Knit

When you begin to work on a pattern placing the first row of stitches on the needle is known as 'casting on'. All further rows are worked into these initial loops. This can be done on one or two needles and the method may be specified in the pattern.

SINGLE CAST ON

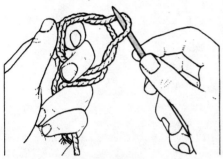

1 Wrap your yarn around two fingers twice and pull a loop through the twisted yarn with a knitting needle.

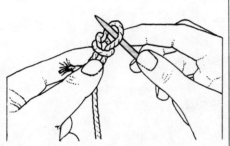

2 Pull both ends of the yarn to tighten. This produces a slip loop.

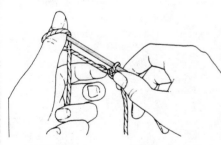

3 With the slip loop on your right-hand needle wrap the working end of the yarn around your left thumb and hold it in the palm of your hand. Put the needle through the yarn behind the thumb.

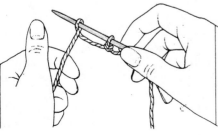

4 Lift the yarn and slide the new 'stitch' towards the slip loop. Tighten the working end to secure the stitch until you have the required number.

TWO-NEEDLE CAST ON

1 With the slip loop on your left-hand needle, insert your right-hand needle through the loop from front to back.

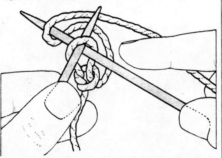

2 Bring the yarn under and over your right-hand needle.

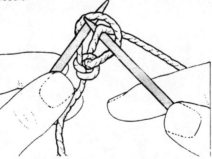

3 Draw up the yarn through the slip loop to make a stitch.

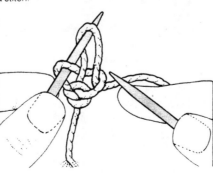

4 Place the stitch on your left-hand needle. Continue to make stitches drawing the yarn through the last stitch on your left-hand needle.

CASTING (BINDING) OFF

When you end a piece of knitting you must secure all the stitches you have finished by "casting off". This should be done on a knit row but you can employ the same technique on a purl row: the stitches, whether knit or purl, should be made loosely. When casting off rib, you must use both knit and purl.

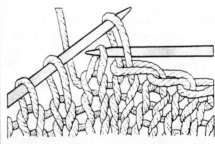

IN A KNIT ROW

1 Knit the first two stitches and insert the tip of your left-hand needle through the first stitch.

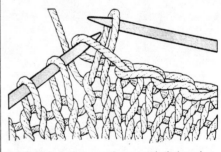

2 Lift the first stitch over the second stitch and discard it. Knit the next stitch and continue to lift the first stitch over the second stitch to the end of the row. Be careful not to knit too tightly. For the last stitch, cut your yarn, slip the end through the stitch and pull the yarn tight to fasten off securely.

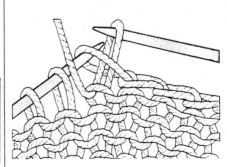

IN A PURL ROW

Purl the first two (and all subsequent) stitches and continue as for knit stitch above.

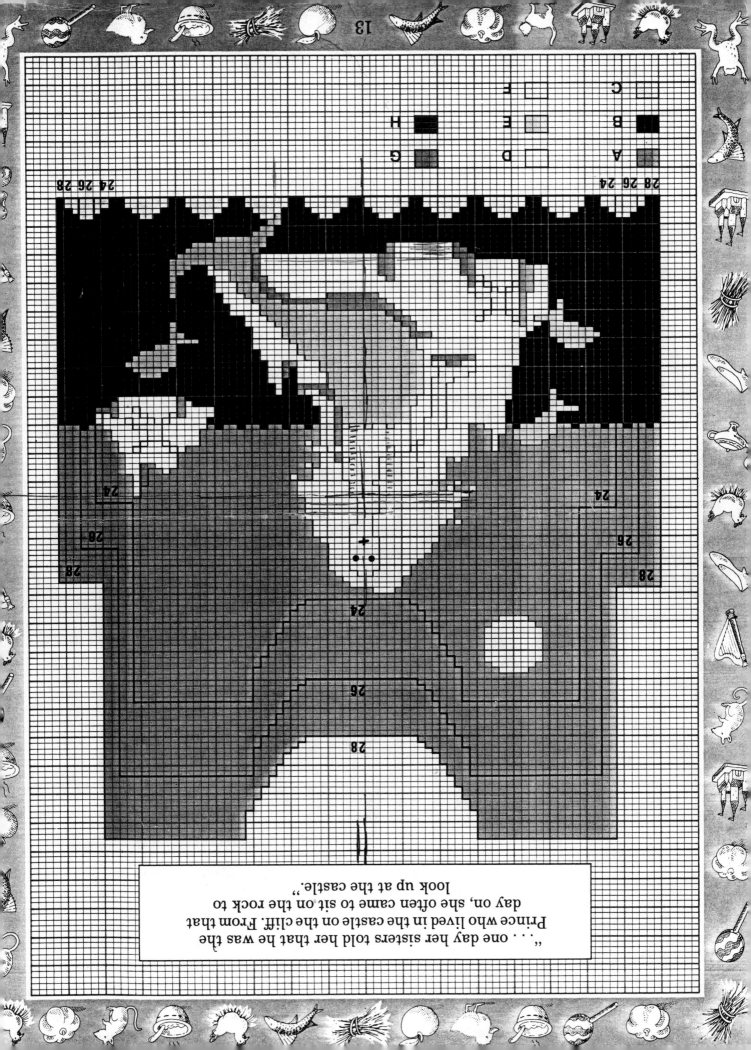

"... one day her sisters told her that he was the
Prince who lived in the castle on the cliff. From that
day on, she often came to sit on the rock to
look up at the castle."